Peoples of
the Sun

OVERLEAF Maya pottery figurine
group showing seated lady with
flower earrings and sleeping boy
with smaller earrings, possibly from
Jaina Island, Yucatan, 9th
century AD.

PEOPLES OF THE SUN

The Civilizations of Pre-Columbian America

C. A. Burland

Weidenfeld and Nicolson
London

Designed by Margaret Fraser
for George Weidenfeld and Nicolson Ltd
11 St John's Hill, London, SW11

Picture research by Pat Hodgson

ISBN 0 297 77136 1

Filmset by Keyspools Ltd, Golborne, Lancs.
Printed in Great Britain by
Morrison & Gibb Ltd, Edinburgh and London

Contents

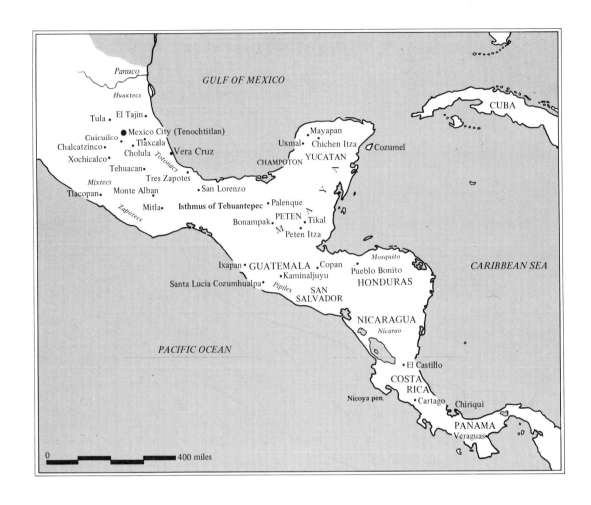

Panuco

GULF OF MEXICO

Huaxtecs

Tula • • El Tajin •

Cuicuilco • ● Mexico City (Tenochtitlan)

Chalcatzinco • • Tlaxcala

Xochicalco • • Cholula • Vera Cruz

Totonacs

CHAMPOTON YUCATAN

Mayapan •

Uxmal • • Chichen Itza • Cozumel

Tehuacan • • Tres Zapotes

Mixtecs

Tlacopan • • Monte Alban • San Lorenzo

Zapotecs

Mitla • • Isthmus of Tehuantepec • Palenque

Bonampak • PETEN • Tikal

M • Peten Itza

Ixapan • GUATEMALA • Copan

Santa Lucia Cozumhualpa • • Kaminaljuyu

Pipiles SAN SALVADOR

Pueblo Bonito

HONDURAS

Mosquito

CARIBBEAN SEA

CUBA

NICARAGUA

Nicarao

PACIFIC OCEAN

• El Castillo

COSTA RICA

Nicoya pen. • Cartago • Chiriqui

PANAMA

Veraguas •

0 ▬▬▬▬▬ 400 miles

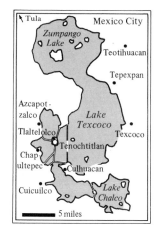

1 The American Indians and their Development

WE MUST BEGIN WITH A MYSTERY. ALTHOUGH WE BELIEVE that the American Indian peoples originally entered the double-continent by crossing the Bering Strait from Siberia to Alaska, we do not know when this movement commenced.

Recently a few Carbon 14 datings of some fifty thousand years ago have been reported from Lower California. However, we know that the last glaciation (the Wisconsin Glaciation in North America) had a continuously variable intensity from very cold to moderately chilly. The glaciation locked up enormous quantities of water in the polar ice-caps, and consequently the ocean levels were lower than at present, more than a hundred feet lower in times of extreme cold. Thus from time to time a wide land bridge existed across the area of Bering Strait. Its width at the maximum was some 150 miles, and on the whole it was not glaciated but was intensely cold. The unglaciated area crossed Alaska and extended down the eastern flank of the Rocky Mountains into the warmer regions of North America.

In such a land there were many animals, from the musk ox, fox, wolf and Arctic hare up to the great hair covered mammoth. There were also caribou and in the seas seals, sealions and many, many cold-water fish in great shoals. This was a world suitable for the human hunter, provided that he had learned how to make himself some kind of footgear and to cover up his bare exposed skin with the furry skins of his prey. Who those first Americans were we do not know. There are a few sites where fires have been lit and heavy flaked stone-scrapers, light flaked knives and heads for darts have been found, but they are earlier than the skeletal remains of ancient Americans. However, it is probable that the first migrants were just one or two families, wrapped in skins, who chased their dinners, the animals, from one continent into another without being aware of any geographical change.

The scanty evidence available suggests that the earliest inhabitants of the Americas were somewhat different from the mass of the more recent American Indians, but in any case the available skulls show that the range of skull forms was as wide in

Olmec stone figure holding a pierced tablet, from La Venta, 8th–9th century BC.

9

ancient times as in modern. There is every reason to believe that the first American Indians were already of a racially mixed stock. The period of their immigration was almost certainly that of the Wisconsin glaciation, which commenced its varied movements some seventy thousand years ago. We have no human traces, so far, from that early period in the Americas. The means of the entry are unknown to us. Maybe some families of hunters entered the continent during a period of extreme cold when they could have marched along the land bridge, hunting as they went. But there is also a chance that some of the primitive hunters came by sea. They had no tools capable of cutting down a tree, but they could cut twigs and saplings, and with these they could make a framework to hold a skin cover. A boat not unlike an Eskimo *umiak* was a possibility for people in a late palaeolithic stage of culture. Thus there is a faint possibility of an invasion of America by sea-hunters working along the edges of the ice sheet. It would be easy enough from Siberia, but the vast oceans would not have made life for invaders from Europe very possible. The parallels between late palaeolithic stone blades from Europe and North America is probably a matter of similar materials fitting into similar needs and thereby establishing a technology quite independent of any culture contacts.

The America discovered by the early hunters was very different from that of the highly civilized Indian communities who are the subject of this book. There were many large creatures which have since become extinct. There is ample evidence from both North and South America that man hunted the mastodon and the mammoth. In the southern continent there is a suspicion that some tribesfolk in Argentina actually corralled a few giant ground sloths in a cave. But the mainstay of the hunters seems to have been the American horse. It was a fully developed horse, rather stocky in build, and roamed the grasslands where it was a source of food for the hunters. There seems to have been no reason why it should not have survived if it were not for the destruction caused by hunting. As it is, the horse disappeared from the scene more than five thousand years ago. Also in the southern continent there were giant camelids, rather like llamas, but they also were hunted to extinction. Similarly, in the northern continent the giant bisons were also driven to destruction, probably by intensive hunting. There has been little climatic change to account otherwise for their disappearance.

The peopling of the Americas probably took many centuries. Recent experience among our few remaining groups of primitive hunters shows that the human community likes to own a hunting territory. It is their homeland, and they usually split into family groups, each working over an allocated region, and then meeting at a selected camping area once a year. They do not move to new hunting grounds unless they are forced to, either by climatic changes or by pressure from other humans. Thus we must allow a long period for the migrations which took a community of hunters as far south as Magellan Strait by a period carbon-dated as nearly nine thousand years ago. This was at Palle Aike Cave, where a family lived on fish and sea animals. But at Fells Cave in Patagonia there was a community of hunters who settled there some eleven thousand years ago. They were already skilled workers in flint, and they chipped projectile points of a fish-tail shape which could be easily bound into split sticks for use as darts. An even earlier group of implements, all delicately flaked, has been found at Pikimachay in central Peru. These may be twenty thousand years old. Similarly ancient tools and animal bones cut by man come from sites in Venezuela. They are outdistanced by some edge-chipped flakes of stone from Chivateros in Peru, which are some fourteen thousand years old.

The story from Mexico and Middle America is somewhat similar. The earliest date so far reported by radio carbon is from the base of sediments at the Valsequillo reservoir in Puebla, where figures around twenty thousand years ago have been ascertained. There was a slow, very slow, development of tool forms until projectile points, probably from darts thrown by a spear-thrower, became common by twelve thousand years ago. Associated with this period a sacrum bone from a giant camelid, rather like a large llama, has been carved into a coyote head, the only example of palaeolithic art work so far known from the Americas. The famous human skeleton, found at Tepexpan in the remains of an ancient swamp in the Valley of Mexico, is now thought to be the bones of a young woman killed during a mammoth hunt. It seems that all the active members of a tribe must have joined in hunting the great beast. But already, at ten thousand years ago, the ancient giant animals were becoming scarce. In the succeeding two millennia they gradually became extinct, the American horse being almost the last to go.

The record is necessarily incomplete, partly because of natural destruction of remains but also by reason of the difficulty of locating sites of such early periods. But it is clear that the whole double continent was, at an early date, probably some thousands of years earlier than any of the dates given above, populated by smallish races of men not unlike the modern American Indians in appearance. They wandered around and around their hunting grounds in small groups of a few related families. A sufficiency of animals, roots and fruits was obtainable. Probably life was happy.

In the colder regions the hunters would have worn some kind of fur wraps, though we must remember that the Fuegians in Darwin's time often went naked or wore only a short fur cape which they moved from shoulder to shoulder to keep off the wind. The tropical tribes probably went naked apart from some paint and feather ornaments.

Judging from recently living hunting tribes, the Palaeo-Indians must have had some simple religious belief about the powers of nature, which were often personalized into legends about the working of the spirit personalities and humans. But we have no actual specimens of tales which seem to come from such far away times. We do know that the tribes acquired increasing skills in flaking and shaping their stone tools and weapons as time went on, but progress was surprisingly slow.

The position of women in such a hunting society was low. It is probable that the facts of conception were only slowly learned, for such hunting communities often supported the idea that children came through a spirit entering the woman and taking form. The pleasures of sex were taken as a joyful experience but were subject to some kind of social control such as marriage, because men were naturally jealous of other men having the pleasure with 'their' women. But life for a woman in a hunting community is hard. There is constant journeying from one temporary shelter to another, no home life and a great deal of difficulty in looking after the babies. Usually the woman in a hunting tribe has to do the cooking, and to find the roots, fruit and edible seeds to eke out the supply of meat.

The world probably owes the invention of agriculture to women. It is strange that the discovery was made at about the same period of about nine thousand years ago both in the old world and in the new. The women of a tribe in the far north of Mexico must have noticed in their continual wanderings that each year they arrived at a place where a small plant bore edible seeds in pairs. Suppose they took some of those seeds and planted others in the earth: the planted seeds might germinate, as they noticed some did which had fallen by accident. The next year was the proof: when they reached the little plantation, they found that the seeds had germinated and produced plants with more seeds. It probably took many centuries before anyone organized life into a true agricultural pattern with regular village life so that women could stay to look after the food plants while the men went out hunting the major part of the diet, from the bodies of the wild animals which they slew. But over those missing centuries of the development of agriculture, women must have continued their old nomadic life wandering with the men round the hunting grounds. The constant search for roots and fruit was hard, and the travelling gave them too little time for their babies. Infant mortality must have been high. In spite of the tribal dances and ceremonies, the women must have been far less happy than the men, and their lesser ability to sustain the long periods of chasing animals made them very junior partners in the family. Yet it is also probable that they held a position as mothers, the bringers of life, which gave them a semi-sacred status. Whether they were the subjects of pictorial art as were the late palaeolithic women of Europe is not certain, since no record of this kind has survived, but the odds are in favour of their being identified with femininity and all creatures which gave birth.

The site from which we have the first evidence of maize in the Americas is in Mexico. The Tehuacan Valley has yielded remains of the earliest maize in the habitation debris on the floor of a cave. At that period maize was a smallish wild grass which produced just two seeds, not the great cobs of recent times. The plant was cultivated with care, and eventually human selection produced a cob-bearing plant which was entirely dependent on human activity for its perpetuation. By the time in which maize was first cultivated, the greater wild animals had mostly become extinct. Whether this had any effect on the cultivation of plant food is uncertain, since the more recent fauna of the Americas could still have provided plenty of food for the hunters as it continued to do among the non-agricultural peoples until modern times.

Other plants cultivated as food in those early days in Mexico were amaranth, which provided a fine edible seed, chili peppers as a relish, avocados with their nourishing pap, and squash which includes the gourds, melons and pumpkins. In later times beans were introduced, and the fruit of the zapote tree was collected. Little by little the development of civilization advanced.

We have no definite date for the first permanent village of little hutments, but its inauguration was the beginning of settled and secure life for women in the community. They had a home and were not required continually to march on the routine trail with the hunters. Probably they acquired a higher status, since their menfolk could hardly fail to associate the Earth as a food producer with motherhood. The children of Mother Earth were not only the animals whose spirits lived in her womb but also her continuous gift of fruit and grain for those who would cultivate her. Even the domestic utensils changed. The baskets and bags of the collectors were replaced with stone bowls which the early villagers of the Mexican plateau fashioned out of steatite. They were magnificent globular bowls which could have served well for the storage of seed corn. It happened between seven and four thousand years ago. Thus the peoples of the Mexican plateau had reached the verge of civilization.

A similar stage was reached far away to the south, on the desert coasts of Peru, as well as in the mountainous highlands. The beginnings of agriculture were about seven thousand years ago, when some of the mountain tribes near Ayacucho began to cultivate seeds and probably domesticated the llama. Other groups of fishing people found an additional vegetable growth on the *lomas* of the coastal desert. These were areas of winter vegetation which afforded a necessary supplement to the diet of the people. Eventually these regions of Peru cultivated edible gourds. In the highlands they domesticated the llama, for wool, skin and meat, and kept guinea-pigs as a safe supply of tasty meat.

The beginnings of village life seem to have been on the coast: at least six thousand years ago a village was made at Quiani on the northern coast of Chile. The inhabitants were fisher-folk, but they visited a nearby river valley to pick up useful rushes and apparently to practise a little agriculture.

Eventually, over some two thousand years of development, the coast of Peru became dotted with villages, all practising agriculture, all close to some well watered river valley coming down from the high mountains. This development reached its maximum between four thousand and four thousand five hundred years ago, and the people by then had added beans and fruit to their diet. In the highlands maize had penetrated from far-away Mexico. Eventually, the villages became overpopulated, and settlements were started in the river valleys where agricultural products were exchanged for sea food. The villages in the valleys became small towns, and quite large buildings were constructed of adobe blocks or rubble.

All the village sites were producing pottery. The skills of the potter may well have developed separately in South America, probably in the mountains behind the Venezuelan coast, where some very early examples of ceramics have been found. The arts spread through Colombia and Ecuador and penetrated to Peru before four thousand years ago. On the Ecuadorean coast villagers of the Valdivia culture were making pottery figures of women, apparently skirted and with neat hairdressing, by about five thousand years ago. It has been suggested that these figurines are evidence of a sea-drift voyage by fishermen of Japan, but the date is quite exceptionally early for the Japanese Jomon culture, and the figures are so simple that it is much easier to accept that they were a local development.

In Middle America, pottery appears about 4,500 years ago. The southern area around Panama seems to have been influenced from

South America, but in Mexico the development seems to have been quite separate. The mixing of sand with the clay to prevent breaking in firing, and the development of the globular bowl forms because the clay pot tends to break in firing at any sharp angle, indicate a longish period of development. In Europe burnt clay figurines were made many thousands of years earlier at Dolni Vestonice in Czechoslovakia, but the hunters mixed their clay with shavings of mammoth ivory, a fatal mistake, so that there was no continuity in production until the much later discovery of sand tempering of clay. The Mexican potters were in fact very skilled, and the fragments of their ceramics show that they could appreciate good shapes in their wares. At Tehuacan and in Guerrero pottery vessels were made, and some fragments equally early have been found in village sites of the Mexican plateau.

There appears to have been no attempt at making a national grouping, and no idea of any basic unity of the American Indian races until the late fifteenth-century development of the Inca idea of Tahuantinsuyu, the Four Quarters of the Earth.

However, the Mexican villagers developed a number of ceramic types which probably reflect tribal differences. An important development of the early Mexican village pottery was the making of little fertility figurines which depict a few male figures and many female ones. They are of high artistic standard in many areas. Probably they served as fertility figures, perhaps made seasonally, for they have been excavated in great numbers from village rubbish heaps, as well as from burials in cemeteries. The men are sometimes draped with a loincloth and are rarely naked. The girls are always naked at this early period and wear most elaborate head-dresses and paint their bodies. Both sexes wear ear ornaments and necklaces which we know were made of clay and hard stone. They show an appreciation of social beauty, and to judge by the obvious determination of the potters to depict elegance of form, we must realize that the early villagers of Mexico appreciated physical beauty.

The houses of the period appear to have been mostly huts made of adobe, either piled up to make a monolithic wall or else built up of large squared blocks used like bricks. The villages cultivated maize and squash, together with chili peppers and fruit, especially that from the Zapote tree. They had many animals – dogs, turkeys and serpents – which caught rats and protected the household.

The settlements on the Mexican plateau are an anomaly in the general context of early American Indian settlement, since they are in open country which has little protection against invasion except the refuge afforded by thickets of reeds in the lake. Almost every other region where incipient civilization appeared was defended either by a desert background or by high and rugged mountain ranges. We can see the dangers to growing civilization in the Americas when we look northwards at the ruins of Pueblo Bonito, a great housing complex which was always under threat from Indians of the great plains. When, in the thirteenth century, a drought made the tribesmen start moving, they attacked and destroyed the settlement so thoroughly that civilization never came there again. Probably there had been several similar tragedies in American Indian history, for the Indians were never united and never realized their essential unity.

The many village sites in the Valley of Mexico were busy places, growing grain, potting, making textiles for their scanty clothing and carving in wood and a little in stone. In particular, at Tlatilco on the outskirts of Mexico City, there was a change late in the second millennium BC, when a number of new pottery forms appeared, vessels with incised designs and, more importantly, large ceramic figures and heads of a different type from the local designs. This was the first hint of a different culture, the first centralized high culture in Mexico, that of the Olmecs. This art links up with the rock sculpture of Chalcatzingo in Morelos where the same strange forms appear in what seems to be its earliest stage. This in itself suggests that the Olmec style was of native Mexican origin and not imported from overseas, for Chalcatzingo is well inland.

However, we must now leave the Mexican area for a while and return to Peru where somewhat similar developments were occurring at around the same period. As in Mexico, civilization developed among the villages. Among the coastal settlements weaving had begun even before pottery-making. Among the fragments retrieved from ruins in the dry desert coastlands are several with ornamental gaps left in the weft. This kind of design element was abandoned for a time, though several centuries later it was revived. The coastal villages specialized in producing twined weaving at first, but by the time they discovered pottery, about four thousand years ago, they had developed a simple back-strap loom with a single heddle which produced fine cloth closely woven. They dyed their llama wool and native cotton with permanent vegetable dyes. As civilization developed, they took to embroidering this over-all weave in bright coloured patterns representing divine beings.

It was only a century or so after four thousand years ago that villagers of the Gaviota period moved up into the river valleys and built small towns, often on stone faced terraces. The tendency was to have a big plaza built up with single-storeyed complexes

Group of Huaxtec pottery figurines of archaic type before 500 BC.

on two or three sides, with a stone and clay pyramid or two on the fourth. Such towns with a population of up to two thousand people were ideal for the development of trade with the coast and for the appearance of the arts. There was already a division of labour, and there was sufficient time for specialists to work on their tasks. There was obviously room for a group of priests, probably a chiefly governor and specialist groups of potters and weavers.

It is clear that by about 1600 BC the coast of Peru was a safe home for several small states, of a few towns on river deltas. They had an organized religion and were technically accomplished. A few made sculpture in stone, but all worked in clay, as both stucco and pottery. At Kotosh, on the eastern ridge of the mountains, ranges of buildings were made on a series of terraces. Many buildings were of stone, but still there were many settlements along the coasts where wooden posts and walls of cane were sufficient cover for the population. Their only experience of moisture in the air was from the winter mists which enshrouded the coast. Rain was a wonder which came only once a century or so. This explains the excellent state of preservation of textiles in the region. There are such quantities of large sheets of textile, often embroidered all over, that one gains an impression of industrious people perhaps working in special rooms at the bidding of tribal officials. Similarly, the size of great pyramids built up of clay and stone suggests a highly organized labour force. At La Florida in Lima, a pyramid was built over a thousand feet in length and a hundred feet in height. It was an isolated building, a ceremonial centre for a number of small settlements. Similarly, the temple edged courtyard at Las Haldas in the Casma Valley was quite apart from civil settlements. Not far away in the same valley at Cerro Sechín religious building includes a wall with incised figures of warriors and their victims. At Kotosh a wall is decorated with plaster symbols of crossed arms.

The earlier pots are all of a grey body. This was probably due to a form of firing in pits, where a heap of leaves on top of the pots prevented full oxidation of the clay during firing. The figures of warriors, and of a sun spirit, are simple incised forms in outline, but colour has been added by mixing powder with resin and baking it on the pot. The colours did not spread because the outlines cut into the surface of the clay presented boundaries.

These coastal cultures were developing well in isolation from other peoples. They had all they needed for a settled life and continued advancement. Maybe they would have amalgamated and built up a larger, more centralized civilization, but this was not to be. Their culture was altered by powerful people from the high mountains in north-eastern Peru. These invaders brought a

Stone head of man from wall of building at Chavín, 9th century BC.

somewhat different religion and a special art style of their own. They came from the headwaters of the Marañon, where they may have been in contact with more ancient cultures to the north. This Chavín culture, named for its famous site at Chavín de Huantar, was fully developed by about 1000 BC and its influence in Peru lasted for some seven centuries. The Chavín sites in the Marañon Basin are not only high in the mountains but some two hundred miles north of the coastal area in southern Peru which they seem to have dominated. The carved patterns on the stone temples in the mountains are so closely related to the designs on coastal Chavín textiles, found particularly at Paracas, that one must postulate a direct influence of such magnitude that a religion was imposed on the coastal people together with its highly specialized art forms.

The art work of the Chavín culture is typically American Indian, in its use of flat surfaces of linear decoration, its insistence on the importance of outline, and the use of symbols which express a story. It is quite clear that the theology behind the art was of a violent character. The constantly recurring themes are the high flying condor, with a tusked mask on every feather of its wide wings, and a grim mouthed earth-jaguar. There are many representations of serpents, perhaps as under-earth powers. The human figures are of squat, long bodied American Indian types, but the faces are usually masks with fierce jaguar fangs, sometimes a whole sequence of masks one above another. Particularly among the coastal peoples we find embroideries of monstrous figures wielding serpents which appear to represent lightning. Some of them fly through the air, carrying human heads in their hands, others walk as warriors carrying clubs and have heads hanging from their garments. These heads look small and so have encouraged the idea that head-shrinking was a Chavín habit, but it is evident from grave finds of headless bodies that the heads represented were simply trophy heads from war victims pierced through the top of the skull for suspension. The makers of coastal Chavín textiles probably paid no special attention to proportionate size, and the figures are more likely to have represented gods than warriors.

The stone buildings of the Chavín culture are strange to our eyes. They were built of carefully squared blocks of stone and were set close among the rocks of the ravines of the Andes. The square faces of the building were slightly battered inwards towards the top, but the sides are not the walls of rooms. The whole form is a solid block in which tunnels and narrow passages have been left. It is a monument which encloses its own underground system of passages and sacred stones. The simplicity of the outer walls is but rarely decorated with heads of men and animals carved in the round and set in position by means of tenons. They are all ferocious of aspect, with bulging eyes and mouths made savage by the inclusion of jaguar teeth. Within the passages there are engraved linear figures and great blocks of stone modelled and decorated with designs which indicate ferocity. In one roof stands a great curved block of stone carved with patterns and a terrifying demon head, as if it were a serpent hanging from the roof. It is called the *lanzon* because it is something like the blade of a lance thrusting down towards the ground. Here are beauty and horror combined. Perhaps it is an image of an earth deity; certainly it is a splendid example of Chavín style art.

The techniques of the Chavín stone workers were essentially simple but excellently well contrived. Blocks of stone were prized from the mountains; sometimes, no doubt, cracks were made by lighting fires on the surface and dousing the red hot rock with cold water. The blocks were prized loose with wooden levers and probably rolled to the building site on sections of tree trunk. The tools used in shaping the blocks were of hard, fine grained stones such as diorite. The fine surfaces of the blocks were hammered out by casting down blocks of stone upon them, pitting them and then scrubbing out the smaller irregularities by blocks of stone as hard as the building blocks. Much hard labour was expended on each block. How they calculated the right angles of the faces is unknown to us, but they were very accurate. Then the blocks were laid together and were cemented, in a clay mortar. This method of construction has preserved the buildings for some twenty-nine centuries in a region noted for its earthquakes. When the tremors occurred, the blocks were thrown a short distance upwards and simply fell back into position. It is probably not a planned system of building, but it worked very satisfactorily. No trace of colour has been found on the buildings, and it seems remarkable that such an artistic people should have missed the value of colour in their symbolic arts.

On the coast the Chavín style is colourful in the embroideries. Buildings are known from the north and south coast and were the usual adobe mixture of clay and sand with a little grass. However, nearly all the material we have is mortuary in character. There are small stone figurines of animals, and the workmen used gold, placer-mined from river beds, to make plaques embossed with Chavín-style figures. These were made into headbands and ornaments sewn onto dresses. The richest expression of coastal Chavín art comes from some later burials in the Paracas peninsula. Here, in deep pit graves, notables were buried. Sometimes the bundles containing mummies were arranged in a ring in a room reached by a shaft, in others a chamber was excavated to take a few bodies also with a vertical well-like shaft leading down. The bodies were dried possibly before burial, and sometimes a primitive mummifying was attempted by the removal of brain and viscera. The bodies were wrapped in fine cloaks, and then great sheets of decorated cloth often fifteen feet by ten feet in size. These were usually of plain woven cloth dyed in a dark rich colour, red, green, brown or black. Then the whole surface was covered by fine embroideries of gods, demons and animals, all in bright coloured cottons. We must consider their possible meanings later when we come to consider the Nasca culture of this coast. The figures of gods and demons derived their forms from Chavín carvings. We meet them as colourful, vibrant forms, holding close to the over-all Chavín designs.

The great sheets of embroidered cloth from the cemetery at Paracas date from about 900 BC to 400 BC. There is no attempt at making a tapestry weave. That was to develop later. At this early stage the huge pieces of embroidery, covered with endless repetitions of divine figures, are testimonies to a social system of an aristocratic kind. They must have been made by a number of women working to a well defined pattern; if one woman had to do the work it would take her many years to cover some two hundred square feet of cloth with complex four-inch squares of figures. Such an expenditure of labour for a burial implies that it was intended for a person of great social importance. The precise nature of the designs implies that there was an over-all control probably from the Chavín area itself, though there is no very clear reason why one of the coastal sites might not have been an administrative capital. From the over-all importance of the divine figures, it must be conceded that a theological element was of great importance. Possibly the chiefs of this growing civilization were the leading shamans who could claim to administer the powers of nature. Perhaps they commanded the armies of whatever tribe they represented; perhaps they led the ceremonies. No legends remain to give us any assurance. But even after the civilization of Chavín had failed in the highland areas, it was alive and powerful in the coasts, and turned into the Nasca culture. Its gold work continued, the paintings on pots reproduced the textile designs, and the textiles themselves developed into fine tapestries.

The basic foods of the ancient Andean and coastal cultures were quinoa, a grain bearing grass, maize, beans and potatoes. In the highlands, hunting of deer and rodents helped out the diet. On the coasts there was a permanent supply of sea-foods: fish, seals and sea-birds. There was no need for anyone to go hungry.

Golden pendant representing a deity with serpent costume, Chavín style, 9th or 10th century BC.

This culture area was cut off from the rest of America by the desert of Atacama to the south and by the great forests to the east and north. There was, however, a seaborne contact by traders in dug-out canoes, which could be made once the tribesmen had acquired the idea of the heavy stone bladed adzes and axes necessary for the work. In northern Peru and Ecuador the balsa tree grew, and its light wood was splendid for rafts, made in something of the same formation as the fishermen's boats made of bundles of reeds. But it appears that the culture contacts with the north were mostly by means of the dug-out canoe.

The canoe was also the means of transport among the peoples of the Amazon and Orinoco basins. They were very few in number until life was well advanced in the neolithic stage, say around 1,000 BC. But then they spread in villages which cultivated manioc, gourds and beans. There was little high culture among them, and the conditions of the country prohibited much advancement, even among the great pottery making areas on the island of Marajó at the mouth of the Amazon. However, along the Caribbean coasts of South America there was more activity, and some lesser civilizations arose along the coasts of Venezuela and Colombia. They made pottery, and it seems that they had contacts with settlements inland which may have been the earliest ceramic making cultures in the Americas. The influences were visible in coastal ceramics in the region of 3,000 BC. In the whole Caribbean area there was a slow movement of population by canoe. Some of the cultivators of manioc had early crossed the Isthmus of Panama and progressed up the Pacific Coast, taking their manioc growing culture together with the essential graters and squeezers as far as southern Guatemala. They were self sufficient to a degree in which they did not take up the maize growing cultures of the highland people. It was a similar situation along the Caribbean coasts of Costa Rica and Nicaragua. This land was rich in gold, but it was not exploited in very early times, certainly not as early as in Chavín in Peru. But art styles found in the time range of 900 to 600 BC show influences filtering down from the Olmecs (more properly the peoples of the La Venta culture, from the type site).

The culture of La Venta begins in the highlands of Morelos around 1250 BC at Chalcatzingo, where a group of rock carvings exist with fully fledged relief sculpture and rudimentary symbols of glyphs. At San Lorenzo, a site in the isthmus of Tehuantepec, another and more important Olmec site has been found. Here sculptures in hard rocks which have been brought from seventy kilometres away have been erected on a high platform of earth also brought from a distance. This great ceremonial area was built up by the labour of a great number of people, probably for

Olmec gigantic stone head from La Venta, between 900 and 700 BC.

religious reasons. The site at San Lorenzo began about 1250 BC, but three centuries later the place was ceremonially abandoned. The great sculptured rocks and eight huge heads were defaced, turned over and deliberately buried. Why? We do not know. Maybe there was war, but the formal burial of the great stones would have taken some time. It was perhaps a ceremonial activity in which a population deliberately moved for ritual reasons. But we do not know. However, on the coast of the Gulf of Mexico, two great Olmec sites remained active until about 600 BC, at La Venta and Tres Zapotes. These dates are Carbon 14 determinations, and until the new corrections by tree-ring dating have been applied, which may make them some three centuries earlier in time, we cannot correlate the moves with the calendrical system.

It is quite clear that Olmec culture was based on a religious rule, and that its influence pervaded all of the civilized regions of Mexico and Guatemala. The system was expressed in an art style which bears a minor resemblance to that of Chavín. In fact the possibilities of contact are present though unlikely. The nature of the religion is, however, similar, since the worship concerned the earth and underworld as opposed to the sky. The sun god is shown emerging from the jaws of earth, carrying a jaguar-faced baby who later leaves his mother and advances with upraised axe to attack an enemy. The carvings remind one of the Aztec story of Huitzilopochtli destroying the stars of the night sky. But there is no legend preserved and little hope of ever finding one, since the few Olmec glyphs seem to have been calendrical.

The introduction of a written calendar seems to have been due to the Olmec. It is part of a parcel of culture traits which are paralleled in south-east Asia and may indicate that there was an irruption of culture bearers from that region. However, one must also consider that there is a common unconscious mind in all of humanity and that people of similar physical type tend to have similar art styles. Whether this psychological matter applies to so many culture traits that it can oppose diffusionist theory is doubtful but possible. So we cannot yet definitely say that the first high culture in Middle America was due to an invasion. The journey, if it did occur, would have been long and difficult, more likely to have been made by one or two boatloads of people than by any great invading force. In any case, how much of culture is likely to be brought in by a few boatloads of wandering fishermen?

The few Olmec glyphs which we have are comparable with the western Mexican tradition, such as Zapotec writing, rather than the Toltec system, but they are few and not certainly deciphered. The art style is remarkable in its combination of sculpture in the

Olmec stone altar with figure emerging with child on lap, from La Venta, between 900 and 800 BC.

round with detail in incised lines. This is splendidly used in the great stone 'altars' at Olmec sites, where emergent figures are in the round as they emerge from the squared stones decorated with linear designs representing the mouth of the earth-monster. A remarkable feature of the Olmec art work is the realistic representation of the human figure: the long bodied, short legged shape, with a high head without much projection at the back, and with thick lips and broad nose, is remarkably like some modern Mexicans of today. A somewhat foolish writer has argued that the typical Olmec head represents a negroid race, but this is entirely fallacious. The black figures on later paintings are of people who by reason of a priestly office have painted themselves black. But the realistic figures of the Olmec are found in stone as three-dimensional carvings and on reliefs. The convention of small and simplified hands and feet on these figures is typically Olmec and is a diagnostic point of equal importance with the facial features.

A very special form of sculpture is the gigantic stone head. Carved in basalt, the three dimensional and realistic heads vary in height from about five feet to nine feet. They are early, to judge by the heads found at San Lorenzo, and they are complete works in themselves. They never had a body or a neck. They occur in the sites of the Olmec heartland, where each was standing quite naturally on a flat prepared surface. One wonders if they represented planetary deities, but this is speculation. Each one of them wears a massive head-dress of straps, rather like an American football player's helmet. Some have a symbol at the front. Perhaps it indicates their quality, but we do not know. As with all Olmec sculpture, the stones were carefully selected and, both at San Lorenzo and La Venta, were carried from some distance away to the site. The sculptors had no metal tools so they battered these realistic heads out of great rocks by beating them and chipping them with stone tools, mostly balls of rock pounded on the surfaces. The linear details were cut with stone chisels, and these were probably made of specially hard stones such as jade.

It seems that these Olmecs were great astronomers, since their use of numeral symbols indicates that they were the first to introduce the standard Mexican calendrical system to the country. Its complexities, due to the constant adjustments between a 360-day *tun* and the astronomical 365 + day year all echo an early origin, just as our 360° circle echoes an even earlier Babylonian count of time. But the ancient calendar of the Middle American people had other corrections which made it in effect slightly superior to our more modern usage. The calendar and its variants have proved to be a useful means of observing the later developments of social groups in the area.

Meanwhile, the Olmecs produced art works, especially a rather coarse and thick pottery which was so characteristic that we can see from its distribution that their influence was spread all over Middle America. One wonders if they organized a military domination of towns and tribes. Some ceremonial objects reflect the sacrifice of prisoners by clubbing. A sculpture at Chalcatzingo shows a group of masked warriors using paddle-shaped clubs to kill a victim seated on the ground, and gods are also seen on Olmec sculptures to carry head masks. If there was a military empire, why was the site of San Lorenzo overturned in the tenth century BC? It seems that after this date Olmec influence is weaker in other parts of Mexico, but the culture continues in its major centres as richly as ever for another three centuries, and sporadic finds of Olmec artefacts suggest that the decline in outlying regions was not so great as has been suspected.

In the field of religion the Olmecs had a deity with a jaguar mask face who might have represented a sun-child. But did they cleave the skulls of children to make the strange visage? They certainly did practise sacrifice. Among their most sacred objects are heavy jade or other crystalline green stone axe blades. They weigh around ten pounds each, and the blade is surmounted by a neck and a blunt hammer top carved in the form of a jaguar mask with a cleft in the middle of the skull. The jaguar mask is carved in full relief and often has a quasi-human aspect. On the front of the blade the arms of the figure are outlined in shallow grooves. The hands support a bar inscribed with an outlined St Andrew's cross. Such a symbol usually indicates the sky, and it is quite possible that the figure represents the sky supporter of the direction of sunrise. One may compare the Aztec myth about the ocelots howling as the sun rises over the eastern mountains and the darkness is slain.

Wherever possible, the Olmecs carved in blue jade, very precisely and beautifully. This implies the rejection of the apple-green portions of jade pebbles, which was later to become the favourite coloured jade of the Maya tribes. The choice was obviously deliberate since the bluish toned jade was also used for pendants, earplugs and specially fine chisels, awls and other tools. The simplicity of Olmec jade work adds greatly to its beauty, and it is realist in intention though conventions give specialized distortions. One notes that the Olmecs also worked in many other hard stones, including the black volcanic glass, obsidian, which they could chip and polish into figurines. One of them was recently immortalized by the painter David Alfaro Siquieros in his picture 'The Echo of a Cry'.

The major contribution of the Olmecs to Mexican civilization was their invention of the ceremonial centre. It was a complex of buildings and usually included a raised structure of pyramidal type. It included banks and ceremonial courtyards all aligned on an axis which in the few examples surviving always points a little west of north, almost as if it were aimed at the Little Bear in the sky. The centre at San Lorenzo was built up from the placing of millions of tons of material, taken from seventy miles away, around a natural hill, to make a ceremonial platform for the monuments. At the type site of La Venta the mass of the ceremonial area was built up of a firm yellow clay brought only a few miles, but it was not the local clay so it must have been regarded as having some specially sacred quality. Inside one courtyard the fill was some twenty feet deep. At about half the depth a very formalized, almost a Teotihuacano style jaguar mask was made in a mosaic of serpentine slabs. This was very carefully laid out, exactly planned for its religious meaning, and then it was covered over, buried under ten feet of sacred yellow clay. This was a quite deliberate act, and its reason escapes us simply because we have no real knowledge of Olmec mythology. In the whole complex there were two courtyards flanked by stone heads and 'altars' and two sarcophagi, one of which was an erection made by columns of columnar basalt broken to make an erection rather like a log cabin without a door. At one end a clay pyramid with fluted sides, some fifty feet high, was erected.

All in all, the Olmecs provide one of the great mysteries of Middle American art. Whence did they come? What was the origin of their glyphic system? How many generations were involved in the development of their calendar? They give us some of the finest sculpture in all ancient American art, and then after about 600 BC, they disappear, leaving an artistic tradition and a new way of life among many people, but no longer remaining as a unitary culture. Were they an imperialist group who were dispossessed by force? Or were they a religious community proselytizing the people around?

The Olmecs departed from power. We do not know the reason why. But they left a cultural bequest of great importance in Mexico. While nothing of direct inheritance remains, there are several cultures in Mexico in post-Olmec times which preserve clear echoes of Olmec styles. Important among these was the site of Kaminaljuyu in Guatemala, where a growing community in what became an important town on the borders of the Maya country built a tomb in which fine pottery and the bodies of a number of sacrificial victims around the corpse testify to wealth and great power. The Olmec culture had undoubtedly left an echo of strange ritual and also of dominant individual chiefs.

Olmec stele showing warrior deity carrying axe and wearing multiple headdress, from La Venta, between 900 and 700 BC.

On the Mexican side of the border with Guatemala, on the western ridge of the mountain chain, was the great town site of Izapa, which was the centre of a new art style for some three or four centuries after the fading out of La Venta. The Izapa style of art still contains echoes of the Olmecs, but it is more complex, and one finds figures wearing bat masks and wind masks in the richly decorated *stelae*. The calendar is the normal Middle American one, and the gods can be equated with the later ones of central Mexico. The town was basically a big ceremonial complex of temples and courtyards which was surrounded by a large and growing area of housing for priests and artisans. It is probable that, on the whole, the town was a ceremonial centre for the great mass of the population living in farming villages after the basic Olmec pattern. Apparently the whole period was one of varied tribal centres, perhaps jockeying for power and never quite succeeding in producing an overall control of the country. One must envisage people of a basic culture, but of several origins, speaking differing languages, with each group holding on to a basically related culture. They were all in the stone age as far as technology goes. In places they organized their ceremonial centres and were rich enough to support a leisured ruling class together with highly trained priests and artisans who worked on ceremonial erections as builders and sculptors. Such centres of culture were at Kaminaljuyu and Izapa. Further north something similar was developing in the valley of Mexico among the villagers there.

The agricultural settlements such as Tlatilco and Ticoman continued in their quiet ways, farming plenty of vegetable food, maize, squash, chili peppers, beans etc. They flourished, and apparently there was an increase in population. At Cuicuilco there had been a much earlier settlement whose medicine-men had built themselves a sacred house out of great slabs of rock arranged in a ring, all sloping inwards like the walls of a domed hut. Perhaps they covered the top with a skin sheet. On the inner face of the stone slabs they had carved in outline several figures, of which the most important was a rattlesnake. In Aztec times the rattlesnake was adored as a symbol of the poverty of mother earth who gave all for her children. We can be pretty sure that the sacred hut at Cuicuilco was on a spot sacred to the earth spirit. Then the years passed. A small village grew into a township with its surround of houses and a temple platform very near the ancient holy place. The settlement grew, and several circular mounds were made and faced with stone. But the central temple was the holy spot. Beside its ruins was found a small squatting stone figure of an old man with a bowl on his head. This was undoubtedly an image of the god of fire, Xiuhtecuhtli. Perhaps he

Large Olmec pottery figurine representing weeping child, *c.* 500 BC. The whole figure is painted over with a white slip.

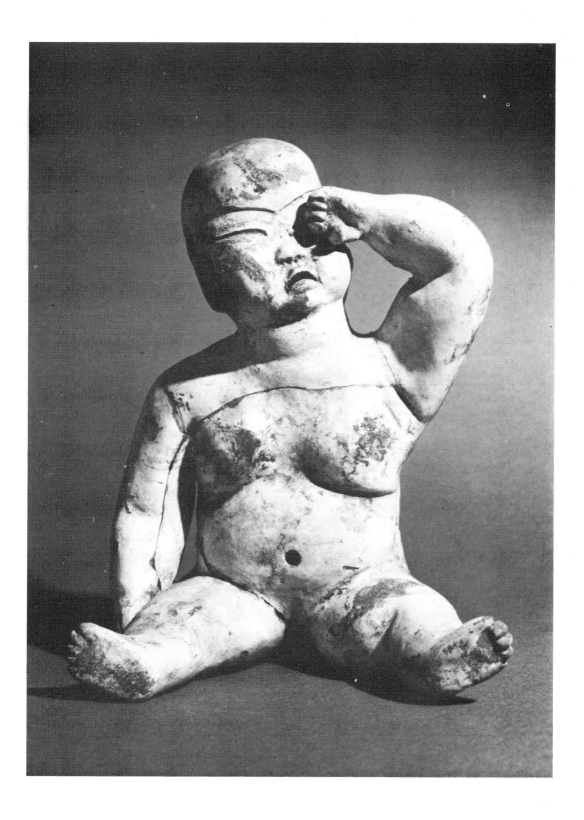

was specially important at Cuicuilco because of a threatening volcano, Xictli, in the volcanic mountains of Ajusco.

The people of Cuicuilco began their town about 900 BC. They left some traces of an Olmec-style baby-faced figure. Also many pots were made, mostly of the local tradition but some in Olmec style. But as the Olmec traditions faded away, the circular temple grew. It was added to at least twice. The core of the conical temple was made of great masses of adobe (clay mixed with chopped grass) and it was faced with stones to prevent the mass collapsing in the rains. The last increase in size was faced with slabs of lava, an indication of a nearby lava flow. The great square, open altar on top was replaced at each rebuilding. It looks as if it had been a fire-altar. But about 350 BC Cuicuilco was abandoned by its people. Probably a particularly nasty eruption had destroyed their fields. But their town had been big enough to have dominated the entire region. After they had moved, no other centre in the valley became so big and important as Cuicuilco had been. But the fate of the place had been sealed. Rubble washed down the pyramid, and the ancient sacred enclosure was left under masses of silt. Then Xictli exploded and from the gap poured a great stream of lava, now solidified to become the Pedregal beside University City. The Pedregal flowed semi-liquid and crackling with fire all over the lower section of the triple staged pyramid, and so sealed in the past one of the most fascinating of the late villages. The eruption is carbon-dated as about 300 BC.

It was not very long after the abandonment of Cuicuilco, at latest late in the second century BC, that another tribal village some twenty-one miles north of the lake built a small mound temple, and then, quite soon, covered it with more and more adobe and faced the mound with stone. This was the beginning of Teotihuacan, 'The Place Where the Gods were Made'. An indigenous high civilization was being born on the Mexican plateau.

Meanwhile, much had been going on in western Mexico. Along the coasts of Honduras, and slowly extending northwards along the Pacific Coast of Guatemala, a people who later called themselves the Pipiles were spreading. They made inscribed monuments in their later stages and carved calendrical inscriptions in what was to become the system used later by the Aztecs. Good potters and keen astronomers, they expressed their culture in splendid sculptured reliefs in a near realistic style. But when they were really a civilized people it seems that Teotihuacan was already past its prime.

In western Mexico, in the area of Oaxaca, a hilltop half a mile above the site of Oaxaca city was carved into open plazas, and

Stone figure of a *danzante*, one of a group of stones showing figures apparently dancing, from Monte Alban, Oaxaca, *c.* 200 BC.

buildings were constructed by a literate people whose carvings resembled in many ways those of the Olmecs. The first settlements at this site of Monte Alban were about 500 BC and were not, at least artistically, Zapotec work, although the Zapotecs settled there and made it a great centre of their culture in the first century AD. The earlier remains at Monte Alban include a building which was faced with carved stone blocks sculptured with human figures in contorted postures. Many of these figures were of bearded men, and some are accompanied by glyphs which seem ancestral to the later Zapotec writing. But the style is close to Olmec art. The figures are all naked, and their sex organs have been slashed so that they curl over the body in writhing curves. It may be that these figures represent sacrificed captives. They were regarded as sacred, since in later times a temple was built over the site, and a tunnel was carefully constructed so that the carved stones should remain free and visible, at least by torchlight. From the glyphs it is quite clear that the Olmec system had developed in this case in the direction of what was to have been Zapotec writing. Further to the south-west it developed into the later Mayan script. On the whole it was probably a syllabic system, as it was to be among the Maya.

Another feature of Monte Alban I art was the manufacture of ceramic urns, mostly of vases in the form of a human head. The grey clay of Oaxaca was used, usually burnished smooth. The faces were not quite Olmec, but many Olmec features remained in them – the ancient tradition was not quite dead, even five centuries after the abandonment of the sacred site at La Venta. Several of them have a headband with decoration either of a three-leaved symbol, related to the later glyph for the Zapotecs, or the band with an x-shaped cross in it, a link with the past.

On the eastern coasts of Mexico, there were other cultures developing quite early in time. At El Tajín the earlier culture belongs to the later centuries BC and developed towards the later classical style of the area. Further to the north, around the mouth of the Panuco River, the Huaxtec pottery tradition began among tribes speaking a primitive dialect of Maya, who must have been separated from their relatives who moved into the Peten and Yucatan at a much earlier date.

When one looks at the material in this chapter, it is evident that there was no unified culture before the Chavín in southern Peru and the Olmec in Mexico. But even in those periods we find many local manifestations around the central areas. There may have been a weak linkage between the two regions, but this is doubtful. The main point to note is that, by 100 BC, the American Indians in these two favoured locations had become settled farmers capable of building splendid ceremonial centres. They appear to have developed social life to the point of division of highly specialized labour, and to have had a well organized religion. This religion was probably different in the two areas, and its apparent grimness may well have reflected the sadness of a mortuary cult in which the powers of death and destruction were linked with the earth. The joy of life and sunshine comes through best in the little ceramic figures made by the natives of the Mexican plateau, who seem to have rejoiced in beauty and fertility.

We must remember that civilization grows but slowly and that in the Americas social conditions probably made it develop in areas where food production was possible and protection from enemies was fairly easy. The twenty thousand years of palaeolithic hunting was a prelude to some three or four thousand years of gradually improving agriculture. Thousands of small tribes lived and died and left their contributions towards the gradual development of a better and richer life. Their reward was that of us all: death. But for those who came afterwards, the beginnings of civilization arrived under neolithic conditions.

We must now turn to the higher cultures in these immense lands, the equivalent of a two-hundred-mile-wide strip of land extending from Great Britain to India in the old world.

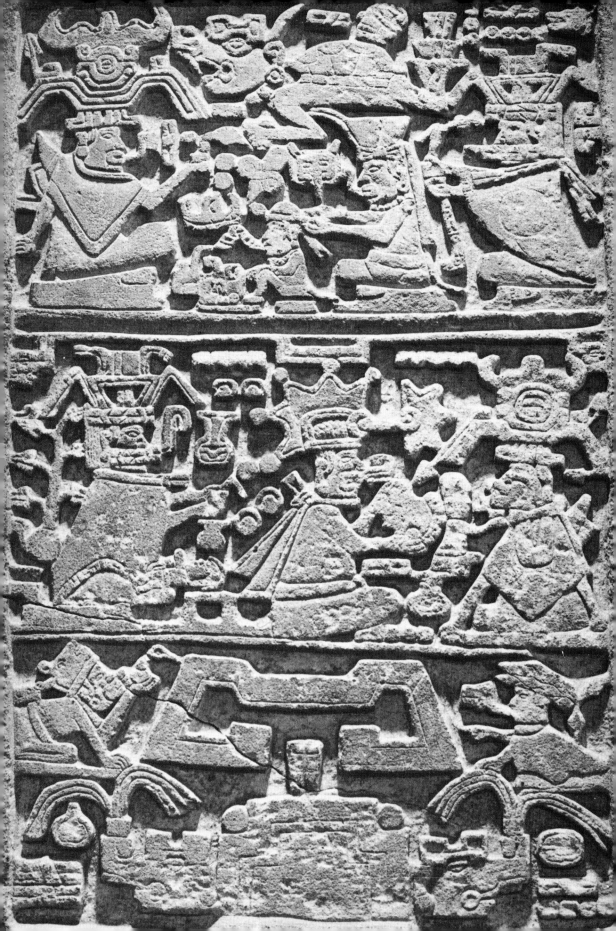

2 The Mexican Development

TEOTIHUACAN AROSE SUDDENLY. IN THE SECOND CENTURY BC, on the dusty plain fifteen miles north-west of Mexico City, there was a small pyramid on which the local tribespeople worshipped their gods. Then suddenly they set to work building another, greater pyramid, the Pyramid of the Sun, over the ancient one. In the clay they used, many old pottery figurines have been found. One guesses that the little things were no longer particularly sacred. The pyramid seems to have been completed in one great effort, for there are no internal divisions. It was as broad at the base as the great pyramid in Egypt but only half as high, and was built in stages with a slightly different angle to each. The total height was two hundred feet. There was a legend that once upon a time a gigantic statue to the sun stood on top, but nothing remains. The whole of the exterior was covered by slabs of stone, but that has collapsed and the remains were removed by the great archaeologist Leopoldo Batres, who removed the rubble but hoped that he had preserved the true shape of the great work. It is an impressive building but how much more splendid it must have been when the real facing stones were there, for it is now restored. We do not know how long this enormous pyramid took to construct, or how many people worked on it. There can be no doubt that it represented an enormous effort by a whole community just to cart the masses of adobe to cover the old building completely. By the building of this enormous monument a little before 50 BC, the Teotihuacanos stated their importance.

In front of the pyramid a processional way was constructed. It was edged by plinths on which stood temples of the gods. At the end of this pathway, but a little to one side, stood the Pyramid of the Moon, not so big as the sun pyramid but still very impressive. Then a great dancing courtyard grew on one side, which could have held thousands of dancers. Beside it was a stepped Temple of the Winds and the Rain which was rebuilt several times in the six centuries of the history of the city. At first there were two sections of the city, but these merged. Finally an area of some six and a half square miles was covered with buildings. The outer ones were but

Carved stele with representations of historical and mythological events from Cuilapan, c. 1000 AD.

huts built on low earthen mounds. In the regions closer to the ceremonial complex there were palaces and several quarters dedicated to priests and skilled craftsmen. Excavations have shown that each craft had its own section of the city. Various estimates of the population of Teotihuacan have been made, and they vary from a hundred thousand to one million. We shall never know the truth. Perhaps the bigger figure would be approximately right for an influx of people at one of the greater festivals.

The food supplies of Teotihuacan depended largely on intensive agriculture and foreign trade. The basic foodstuffs were amaranth seeds, maize, squash, tomatoes etc., while meat was provided by turkeys, wild pigs and a few deer. The site, about fifteen miles north-west of Mexico City, had easy access to the shore of the lake, some five or six miles away, so water-birds and fish were available. The layout of the outer house-mounds is well spaced, so that each home probably had its garden. The centre of the town was devoted to religion, and that religion was predominantly agricultural. It was a well drained area with underground drains under the courtyards, especially those which gently sloped downwards below the main processional way. The areas of priests' houses are important, for the walls are frescoed, as far as they remained standing after the destruction of the city. The frescoes depict gods, mostly aspects of Tlaloc, Lord of all Sources of Water. Nearly all the figures spread their hands and pour out streams of water and seeds or jewels. The gods were the givers of life and pleasure. Above them all the rain god ruled, and he was wrapped in an elaborate theology. Some of the paintings show that the god on earth was a manifestation of some great heavenly bird, which in turn was inspired by a bright-eyed magical being in a higher sphere, sometimes surrounded by stars.

These fantastic frescoes belong to Teotihuacan III, the great period of the city, in the third and fourth centuries AD. It appears that now it had a wide dominion over Mexico. Teotihuacano art is represented by pottery, sculpture and painting styles, as far south as Kaminaljuyu in Guatemala whence it influenced growing Maya arts, as far west as Monte Alban in Oaxaca, where the majority of buildings showed echoes of Teotihuacano architecture, and even in the north-east, where the styles of design among the Maya-speaking Huaxtecs reflected the art. Presumably the 'empire' of Teotihuacan was held down by military means: we find occasional pictures of warriors, as well as great numbers of arrowheads and spear points flaked from obsidian. But the betting is that the real power was exercised by a divine ruler, a priest king perhaps rather like the Uija Tao of the Zapotecs. The

OPPOSITE Stone figures which supported a pyramid erected to the Toltec deity, Quetzalcoatl, between 7th and 9th centuries AD.
OVERLEAF Pyramid of the Sun photographed from the top of the Pyramid of the Moon, Teotihuacan, 7th century AD or earlier.

Olmec jade figure covered
with jaguar symbols,
9th or 10th century BC.

whole evidence of archaeology stresses the vital importance of religion and the depth of the theology of the Teotihuacanos. In the great city we find very little that seems like a secular palace. The great houses were sacred places for priests to live and debate among the religious frescoes.

One can trace the development of the Teotihuacanos in the sequence of their clay figurines. The earliest ones have delicately modelled tiny faces and rhythmic bodies which look for all the world as if they were the dancers in the fresco of the 'Earthly Paradise' painting in Tetitla. The necks are fragile, and often we are faced by heads alone. These people wear very simple clothes, loin cloth for a man and a wrap-around skirt and a cape for a woman. By Teotihuacan II we find the faces are much more realistically modelled, and clothing becomes more elaborate in material, with much more decoration. Some of the little images wear face paint of a type found in the wall frescoes. Women's clothing is often decorated with fringes; men wear more elaborate head-dresses. By IV we find more elaboration but rather weaker modelling. The images of gods found in III proliferate in IV and become at once more elaborate and artistically weaker.

The Mexican archaeologist and art historian Laurette Séjourné has identified many of the gods of Teotihuacan with the gods worshipped in later times in Mexico. She has shown that although Tlaloc was the major deity, many other spirits appear: the corn god, the god of suffering, the lord of the winds and several goddesses. We cannot name them properly since we have no evidence of the Teotihuacano language. But it is quite clear that the Teotihuacanos worshipped a typical Mexican pantheon, although their very individual style in art differentiates their work from all other Mexican cultures.

The sculptures of Teotihuacan are all of a cubic tendency. A squared block of stone has been worked on all four sides, and each side presents a flat picture of the deity, though all combine as aspects of a solid figure. An excellent example is the giant figure of a goddess, now in the National Museum of Mexico. Another example is a smallish calcite figure of an ocelot, in the British Museum, which was used as a receptacle for small offerings. The mask of the animal and its paws are formalized to the point where it is clear that they represent glyphs used for writing.

We have no examples of Teotihuacano writing apart from calendrical symbols, and some sequences of symbols associated with the gods and their gifts. It is clear that such a great and powerful civilization must have employed writing, but probably all documents were painted on paper or leather which has disintegrated in the course of time. Even inscribed pots rarely display more than one or two symbols which are probably glyphs. This is strange, since the contemporary Maya peoples were busy writing calendar inscriptions on stone and pottery, and at Kaminaljuyu in Guatemala a great Teotihuacano town was trading with the Maya.

It appears that the Teotihuacano hegemony spread over Middle America in the normal piecemeal fashion. They greatly influenced, though probably did not dominate, some of the surrounding peoples, such as the Totonacs of southern Vera Cruz and perhaps the Zapotecs of Oaxaca. But the general forms of architecture of these peoples and some of the masks on figures are distinctively Teotihuacano in style. The general art style, however, is different in quality from the true Teotihuacano tradition. But in all other parts of civilized Mexico, from the Guatemalan Highlands to the Panuco River and through the Pacific coast, there is ample evidence that art work was widely distributed so that it is wise to suppose the existence of a Teotihuacano dominion. One must suppose it to have been a predatory system of exacting tribute from subjugated tribes, much as was the case in later Aztec times.

The most outstanding products of Teotihuacano art are the stone masks of the gods. These are made of many stones, usually of dark green serpentine. In one case a great deal of a covering skin in a small mosaic of jade, turquoise and shell has remained, showing that they were covered in colours which showed which of the deities they represented. In any case the corners of the eyes and mouth have been drilled to accommodate inlaid eyes and teeth. The backs of the masks have been hollowed out, and it looks as if they had been made to fit onto wooden bodies of figures. Perhaps as in Aztec times, the masks of the gods were changed around as their aspects changed with the seasonal ceremonies. There are usually two perforations at either side of the flat top of the mask, and they could be used for suspension or for attaching a head-dress. From the paintings it appears that the masks were mounted on costumed figures and surrounded with ornaments in elaborate and brightly coloured featherwork which emphasized the meaning of the deity shown.

The main source of information about the spread of Teotihuacano hegemony is the very distinctive ceramic style. There are high broad-necked vases and a great variety of figurines and bowls, but the main line of Teotihuacano potting was the cylindrical vessel with three short feet, either solid or hollow. The walls of the vessel usually curve inward from the vertical, and this is the natural result of firing when the walls were thin. Usually the surface has been burnished after the application of the

The Pyramid of the Sun at Teotihuacan, 1st century BC. The structures in the foreground are part of the ceremonial way, The Street of the Dead, 2nd or 3rd century BC.

dark red slip which is typically Teotihuacano. Such vessels sometimes have incised decorative patterns on the sides, and quite often they include a glyph or two, or even a drawing of a god's head, which reflect contemporary Maya work. A special variety of these cylindrical vessels is covered by fresco. These vessels could not have been handled a great deal; probably they were kept in temples or other safe places. The whole surface was covered with a thin coating of fine, hard white plaster. This was then incised with a design, usually of a god, and painted in watercolour. The colours are pale, mostly a gentle pea green,

Small pottery figure of a man or god wearing ceremonial ornaments and feathered headdress, from Teotihuacan, 1st century AD.

LEFT Frescoed vase showing the rain god Tlaloc seated above a planet and star eyes, from Teotihuacan, 3rd or 4th century AD.

ABOVE Wall painting from a priest's house at Teotihuacan, 3rd century AD. It represents an ocelot, crying for the blood of sacrifice shown just below its mouth.

LEFT Huaxtec pottery vessel in the form of a painted lady, *c.* 7th century AD.

white, yellow and the soft magenta-pink of the city's art. Here we have an example of co-operation between the expert potter and the skilled painter and plaster-worker.

The houses of the city, as far as they have been excavated, included an area of sacred quarters in which priests seem to have lived. The palace at Zacuala, excavated by Laurette Sejourné, was a case in point. There was a complex of rooms and courtyards. The inner walls, as far as they remained, had been covered with frescoes, in the arrangement of unusual colours which marks Teotihuacano art. Many of the figures of the gods could be identified with later deities. It appears that most of the rooms opened out onto a courtyard. They had square pillars at the open end so that the rooms were full of a cool light. Unhappily, the city had been destroyed by violence, so the houses had been packed with the debris of the roofs and upper parts of the walls. But what remained was splendid. In the same area were graves: circular pits in which the dead had been placed in a squatting position with fine pottery around their feet.

A similar complex of painted buildings has been uncovered at Tetitla, also a part of Teotihuacan. Here was the famous fresco of the Earthly Paradise, where the spirits dance among butterflies and play with plants and each other. It is a scene of great happiness, as if the otherworld of the Teotihuacanos were not a place to be dreaded, at least by those called by Tlaloc to inhabit his world of rains and rainbows. These painted houses with their religious message that the gods provided both food and beauty and demanded sacrifice, make it clear that Teotihuacan, despite its unusual art style, was thoroughly Mexican. The great city was the symbol of power for the period. Its riches and glory were stupendous in that world, and its warriors and tradesmen travelled far, bringing in tribute for the glory of Tlaloc and the fertility deities. Even the rituals of sacrifice seem to have been established. There are many pictures of hearts dripping blood and of sacrificial knives. In one pottery figurine in the British Museum a human victim stretched over a stone offers his own heart in sacrifice. Such sacrifice had a glorious aim, to bring fertility and life force to the land in exchange for a few human lives.

One cannot estimate the antiquity of heart sacrifice in Mexico; it may have occurred in Olmec times, but no overt representation is known. However, it was a great force in Teotihuacano life and is represented in the religious art quite strongly. But also there was another spirit, the Morning Star which prefigured the later Quetzalcoatl and presumably represented the idea of a god opposed to blood sacrifice for whom the acceptable offerings were fruit and flowers. This is not a confusion but an expression of the

Stone column with the mask of the rain god Tlaloc, from Azcapotzalco, 6th century AD.

importance of opposites in religious mythology. Such a duality becomes clear for the first time at Teotihuacan. It is clear that the entity which we call Mexican culture had come into being and flowered strongly in this mighty imperial city.

In the south, at Kaminaljuyu, the Teotihuacano traders were in close contact with the Maya tribes, and one finds traces of the art and ideas of both peoples on a number of objects. Some Maya *stelae* include Teotihuacano figures, and some Teotihuacano pots have decorations in Maya style. Nevertheless, there is little evidence of a real uniting of cultures. It seems that we have a great city, on the outskirts of modern Guatemala City, which was primarily a trading community and which did not assume political control over any group of Maya Indians.

Further north, in the mountains of Oaxaca, we have the remarkable case of the Zapotecs. This nation had its own language, strongly tonal in structure, and it survived down to the last days of Aztec power at the end of the fifteenth century. As Teotihuacan rose to power, the arts of the Zapotecs at Monte Alban changed. The works, particularly in the period of the third to fifth centuries, which we call Monte Alban III, were very greatly influenced by Teotihuacan. The temple substructures were ascended by stairs, on either side of which were basically sloping faces surmounted by recessed panels of stonework. This was typically Teotihuacano in style. Much of the facing of these stone-built structures was covered by fine plasterwork, but none of the painting on it has survived.

Tombs were much more elaborate than those of the Teotihuacanos. They tend to be neat underground rooms with a doorway over which was ranged a group of pottery urns with figures of gods. Presumably these were the guardians of the dead. Within the tomb the body was laid on the floor covered in ornamented textiles, of which a few stone beads and ornamental panels have survived. Sometimes a raised ledge also held several more of the elaborate figure vases. Its back and the sides of the tomb were often painted with a plaster-backed fresco.

These frescoes present processions of priests and possibly gods. The costume is richer than in Teotihuacan, and most of the figures wear thick skirts and capes in rich colours. Notables wear most elaborate head-dresses reminiscent to some degree of those of Teotihuacan. They are built up to represent the heads of jaguars, bats and birds, presumably made of wood or cane with coverings of cloth and fine feathers. The use of great quantities of featherwork is quite typically American Indian. Prominent among them are the tail feathers of the Quetzal bird, long and of iridescent green. In fact green is the predominant colour in these

Zapotec frescoes, though the background is white. In some of the tombs the figures are large, shown as great masses of colour with clear outlines to the shapes. They are rather frightening in this aspect of gigantic flowing creatures. Perhaps the beings of the underworld are represented here, surrounding the dead.

In the period Monte Alban III, from the third to fifth centuries AD, the ceramic funerary urns are typically Zapotec in their treatment of ornament and costume, but the facial features of the seated figures are thoroughly in the style of Teotihuacano art. In some cases these great grey urns were covered with a pale base colour and then painted in colours which have now mostly disintegrated. But some of the darker vases were coloured a rich deep red with a powder colour which has remained in all inward facing corners of the design.

These funerary urns are remarkable works of art and come from all periods of Zapotec culture, though the style varies with time. Basically they begin as a cylindrical vase, flat based and about ten to fifteen inches in height. On this broad strips of clay have been luted to form the ornamental costume, and modelled sheets in full relief mark face, torso, hands and feet. Any potter will agree that it is very difficult to arrange such structures of sheets and areas of clay so firmly that they will not flake off during firing. But the Zapotec potters made these religious figures very securely, and although many are partially broken, nearly all were firm and intact when they were buried. It is not clear whether the open vessel at the back, which forms the core of the figure, was ever filled with grain or liquid. The basic clay, however, is slightly porous. Its colour varies from grey to rich black. The tempering material is sand or crushed rock, added so that the clay should contract less and not crack in firing. The common pattern of a group represents a major deity of larger size flanked by smaller figures, often wearing rain-hats which slope from above the head to the shoulders. Many of the major figures represent the great Zapotec rain god Cocijo, an analogue of Tlaloc. But one also finds many more gods. One wears a dog-like mask, and he may well be the Evening Star, who sends the sun down into darkness and is therefore an appropriate funerary deity. Others represent a plump-faced young man with stripes on his cheeks, possibly a solar deity, and there are several feminine deities, who probably represent the goddesses of flowers and of the underworld.

The figures on the urns tell us a lot about costume. Although it is the usual Mexican pattern of loincloth and sandals for men and wrap-around skirt and cape for women, there is a rich field of decoration which makes them stand apart as Zapotec work. However, the head-dresses tell a richer story, since they are usually fronted by a symbol which tells us more clearly the nature of the god represented, and they extend into decorative wings. One splendid example is surmounted by a great bird, possibly a symbol of the planet Venus, but more like the Moanbird of the Maya, an owl-faced creature, than like the Quetzal bird of Quetzalcoatl in later times.

There was undoubtedly an educated class of priests among the Zapotecs. Some among them might have designed the great ceramic urns, but on the whole Zapotec pottery was made by women. There must also have been a military class, probably with some specialist commanders but mainly a militia of all young men in the tribe. They were a dour people, very strongly traditional in their ways. They preserved the ancient institution of divine kingship right through to their defeat by the Aztecs at the very end of the sixteenth century. Although probably not conquered by either the Teotihuacanos or the later Toltecs, they were greatly influenced by these cultures. Their scientific achievements were basically of the usual Middle American pattern of astrology. They built a very useful observatory on Monte Alban with passages and openings for the exact observation of the stars and planetary movements. No doubt this building was primarily consecrated for the purpose of keeping a time-table for work on the farms. On its outer walls there are incised symbols which are mainly place names in Zapotec style.

Though their language was tonal in structure, they used a system of writing in symbolic glyphs, of which the calendrical signs were finally deciphered by the late Dr Alfonso Caso. Probably the other symbols may have denoted words or syllables, with different symbols for the different tones given to the sound, but of this we cannot be certain. As in all Middle American calendars, the days were twenty in number, and they combined with thirteen numerals to form a magical period of 260 days which was used for prognostication. But the year consisted of 365 days made up of $20 \times 18 + 5$ days.

Thus there is a framework within which Zapotec historical documents, mostly carved on stone *stelae*, could be fitted. But the record is not continuous, as it became in the painted books of their neighbours the Mixtecs. However, Zapotec culture continued right through the upheavals of Mexican tribal history, and indeed it survives today in great measure. The great President Benito Juarez, who expelled the French invaders, was a pure-blooded Zapotec. Probably the mountainous nature of their country assisted the continuity of their culture. It was only once threatened when in the eleventh century the great Mixtec chief Yac Quaa (Eight Deer) Ocelot Claw defeated them in battle after battle and finally forced the Zapotec high chief to surrender at Mitla when Mixtec forces had already penetrated to the Pacific shores. But in the painting in Codex Zouche-Nuttall in the British Museum we find that the conqueror revered the conquered Zapotec chief as a living god.

The Mixtec peoples apparently lived in their high sierra country throughout the times of the Teotihuacano hegemony. However, they do not enter history until the very end of the sixth century when Teotihuacan was approaching its end, if that had not already taken place. They became an element in the rule of the later Toltecs of whom we shall hear more in the next chapter.

On the coasts of the Gulf of Mexico the Teotihuacano period saw the development of two very diverse cultures, those of the Huaxtecs and the Totonacs. Both were peoples highly skilled as sculptors, and so we have some record of their beliefs. But they were very different as far as style goes. Also they differed in language. The Huaxtecs were speakers of a language related to the Maya far away to the south. Probably they were the remnants of a widespread people who had been split apart by later invasions from the highlands.

The later Aztecs despised the Huaxtecs because the men went naked and the women were bare above the waist. Their nudity was due mainly to the high humidity of their tropical coasts, but they tempered it by stamping their skins with patterns in black and painted areas of colour. Such patterns were painted on their buildings, and as one becomes used to the massive forms, they develop into figures of gods and animals. But it is a unique art form quite characteristic of the Huaxteca people. The black colour was made from native oil seepages from the rocks around the mouth of the Panuco River, now the great petroleum region of Mexico.

The Huaxteca did not leave many great architectural monuments, but their sculptured figures are of importance to the study of Mexican beliefs, because their images of the gods show that they were the first to present the gods of the Toltecs and Aztecs in their classical form. In particular they show Quetzalcoatl, the Morning Star, wearing his symbolic wind-jewel made of the end section of a large conch shell. His symbolic serpents coil around him, and he wears a typical Huaxtec hat, a high crowned sombrero. We also find great high columns of natural shaped stones which are carved with the figure and symbols of the holy Quetzalcoatl, the Morning Star. This is of course natural, since the coasts of the Huaxtec country were eastward facing, and so the morning star was easily visible, rising from the sea before the sun. This Huaxtec art spans the period of late Teotihuacan and all the

Front (*left*) and back (*opposite*) of a Huaxtec divine figure representing life and death, between 10th and 14th centuries AD. The skeleton figure is worn on the back of the god. Its clawed feet indicate that it shows an earth deity and the pattern on the figure represent typical Huaxtec tattooing.

Pottery figure of a Totonac lady wearing a skirt, cape and headcloth, from southern Vera Cruz, between 11th and 13th centuries AD. In real life the discs on her cheeks would have been applied with a pottery stamp.

Toltec period. Its influence penetrated Aztec tradition in the story that when the Shadow, Tezcatlipoca, wished to destroy the Toltecs, he appeared in Mexico as a naked Huaxtec trader. His painted body, especially his beautiful penis, so attracted the royal Princess that she pined until her father permitted her to marry the man. Thus she became mother of the last Quetzalcoatl of the Toltecs under whom the empire disintegrated in civil war.

Huaxtec art is best shown in their pottery in which human and animal figures are coiled from ribbons of prepared clay, smoothed and then painted in black. It is from the pottery figures that we learn most about the tattoo patterns favoured by the people. The human figures in clay represent a chubby and even fat race of

Indians who all wear a simple headcloth to protect against the sun.
There are also a number of pottery vessels in the form of a dragon-
headed toad, perhaps the earth monster. They are well rounded,
and the neck and head project to form a spout. There are several
other vessels, well rounded, which have a high spout in front and
a shorter one behind, which made pouring through a narrow
spout easier since air entered at one end as the liquid flowed from
the other. A good many of these almost globular vases were
slightly modelled and fully painted to represent human heads,
though, as most of them have their eyes open, we cannot say that
the Huaxtecs were head-hunters. In fact they were addicted to
singing and dancing, and had a great liking for gambling with
beans or pebbles on a board for the game *patolli*, which was not
unlike our ludo.

One cannot doubt that the Huaxtecs were a subsidiary of
Teotihuacan, but their culture continued on its own path long
after the fall of the Teotihuacano domination. Even the dominating Aztecs in later times admitted that the Huaxtecs were living in
the homeland of many of their greatest gods. However, in Aztec
times the importance of the Huaxtecs had declined considerably,
perhaps because of limitations in the productivity of their
country.

To the south of the Huaxtecs, but also a coastal people, lived the
Totonacs. These were much more advanced culturally. They also
overlapped the period of Teotihuacano domination. At first a
nation of agriculturists, making pleasant pottery figurines, they
developed their towns largely under the influence of Teotihuacan, making the usual pyramidal temples and using their own
versions of the recessed panels over a sloping base in each stage of
the building. Their area, at the eastern shore of the isthmus, made
them sensitive to all the cultural influences spreading from the
isthmus. But they developed a great deal of trade in the tropical
products of their country, which included large quantities of
cocoa beans. Their mineral wealth was important since they
controlled some of the hill country from which in more ancient
times the Olmecs had found boulders of true jade. This was an
important and valuable material, both for trade and, even more
importantly, for its magical qualities of life.

They were always in contact with the Maya peoples to the
south, probably trading a great deal with them, especially with
the people of the city of Palenque which was within a few days'
journey across some rather difficult river crossings. This may well
explain certain Maya features in the design of their art work.
However, as time went on, the powers of Teotihuacan declined,
and the isthmus of Tehuantepec was the scene of a cultural change

coming from the west. At least this seems to be the reasonable explanation of artistic elements of unusual type found on the western coasts of Guatemala and also the Totonac cities on the Gulf Coast. This cultural influence includes great numbers of *hachas*, flat slabs of stone rather square in outline but probably meant to be mounted in a cleft stick like an axe head. Many of them were carved into faces. A number of these *hachas* were found in the ruins of smallish hutments built within the great ceremonial buildings at Palenque, which were abandoned in the eighth century, well before any other of the great Maya cities had fallen. Thus it seems clear that the people who made the *hachas* in the region of the Totonacs also caused the destruction of the Maya site at Palenque.

However, soon after the failure of Teotihuacan, the Totonac city of Tajín became more important. Its temples spread and included the Temple of the Niches, which was built with 365 niches, each of which probably contained some figure or symbol of the god of a day. Sculpture from the walls of the town included considerable areas of very low relief figures representing ceremonial events. This work was often made more distinct by the use of double outlines and a type of scroll work which is definitively Totonac. Part of this style of art survived in an ancient page at the introduction of Codex Laud, which otherwise belongs to Aztec times. The walls at Tajín show scenes of sacrifice to the gods. The figures wear some strange ornaments, which are very like the famous Totonac art objects called *palmas* and *jugos*. These seem to be the symbolic decorations of players in the sacred ball-game, and again they link up with the costume of certain figures from the Pacific coast which wear the *jugo* around their waists.

The elaborate decoration of these small-scale objects in stone is one of the glories of Totonac art. We find symbols, figures, animals and vegetable motifs, carved in high relief, with all area surfaces edged with a raised beading, giving the characteristic double-outline aspect. They reproduce the figures of a theology which is close to the standard beliefs of the Aztec period. It is only the artistic style which differentiates the later Totonac culture from the religious art of the Toltecs and Aztecs. In pottery too, the Totonacs distinguished themselves by fine modelling. They made large figures, squatting in posture and nearly realistic in style. In these the men wear the standard loincloth and the women a wrap-around skirt to just below the knee, but their breasts are bare. The exact modelling shows that these tribes respected physical beauty and emphasized the quality of skin and form. Even the figures of old people, such as a famous statue of the fire god, show a quality

Totonac ceramic figure of a singing girl wearing a skirt and ornaments of shell, from Vera Cruz, between 10th and 12th centuries AD. Her headdress, probably originally made of wood, indicates a linkage with creation.

of smooth musculature, observed from nature, and a beauty of surface, in spite of shrunken limbs.

The richness of decoration and the whole quality of Totonac sculpture makes this region one of the great centres of Mexican art. It appears to have been one of the main centres of belief in the country. But it owed much of its ideology to influences from all around. The Huaxtec gods were there; the equipment for the ball-game came from the Pacific Coast; the sculptural art was related to that of Xochicalco in central Mexico. But Xochicalco was an ancient town, having its origins in the full Teotihuacano period. It had lasted for some centuries. Amid its ruins almost the last great building was the famous temple, the truncated pyramid decorated with enormous reliefs of the feathered serpent along its sides and Maya-like figures squatting within the undulations of the serpent. There is a linked date on this monument which marks the short period of eight days' invisibility of the planet Venus in the Mexican calendar system. This is about 580 AD. This temple late for Xochicalco has an art style and a calendrical system like that of the later Toltecs. It indicates that there was another civilized culture at work, entering the southern region of the Mexican highland zone. The figures of the serpent are marked with double outlines, in the main similar to the arts of Tajín.

An apparent blockage to the spread of the common artistic impulse of western Mexico, Tajín and Xochicalco, the impulse which forced the untimely evacuation of Palenque in the Maya region, was due to the great city of Cholula. This was the centre of the worship of the Morning Star, Quetzalcoatl. He was worshipped all over Mexico; his symbol, the five-pointed wind-jewel, and his homonym the Quetzal-serpent decorate many great buildings. But at Cholula he had his holy house on top of a pyramid. This great mound housed an ever-increasing complex of buildings. It was refaced and increased in size at least every 104 years, probably every fifty-two. The archaeologists have excavated tunnels through the great complex and exposed wall after wall, some with decorations. They were once the outer faces of pyramids which had been built up one over the other as time and the importance of the pyramid temple had increased. There are evidences of constant growth, and the art styles reflected the changing cultures which had dominated Mexico from time to time. The Aztec tradition in 1520 was that Cholula had been built by a people called the Olmeca-Xicalanca. But at so late a date mythology and history had become mixed, and we cannot disentangle them. It may be that a rubber-growing people who would naturally be called Olmeca had been there. Certainly some of the remains of fresco on the innermost pyramid are somewhat Olmec in type, but we know that Olmec is probably not the real name of the first civilized people in Mexico. It may be that the Teotihuacanos were called Xicalanca, but we have no proof. However, that Cholula was a holy place in Teotihuacano times is proved by the buildings of the period. It also formed a part of the later Toltec imperium, but after the fall of the Toltecs Cholula remained a great city, the centre of the worship of Quetzalcoatl, until it fell to the Aztecs. Even then it was a holy city and socially very important.

This mighty city of Cholula, sometimes an independent state and sometimes subject to a dominant power, was probably as solid an inhibitor of radical change as were the Zapotecs in

Pottery head of a Totonac
girl with characteristic
hairbraids, from the middle
Gulf coast, after 10th
century AD.

western Mexico. It was there; its culture was very stable; and it
was a unifying force through the ages because it was a pilgrim
centre for all the people of Mexico. It wielded a considerable
military force because its militia were numerous, but it was never
an imperial city. Rather, it was a great place for trade because of its
many contacts across the country, and its markets were usually
full. Thousands of pilgrims came to climb the myriad staircases to
its assemblage of temples on the sacred mound, which was the
largest man-made structure on earth. At the top a circular
building was the home of the god, where he could forgive sins or
inspire fertility. He was the most beloved of the Mexican deities,
though lacking in apparent power when compared to the great
demi-urge Tezcatlipoca, the Trickster, whose name means Smok-

ing Mirror. But in Cholula Quetzalcoatl reigned supreme. Now his temple mound is surmounted by a charming little Catholic church, and the ancient stairways are eroded away. Only the ancient temples under the powdery mass of rubble which makes up the mound remain.

Mexico in the first six centuries of our Christian era was dominated from Teotihuacan. The Aztecs were probably correct in naming the great ruin field with its huge pyramids 'The Place Where the Gods were Made'. Towards the end of its power the arts had become rather more florid, and the wealth of its people had produced much more magnificence in costume. The city was a glorious centre of an agricultural religion, centered upon the rain and water god, Tlaloc, without whose grace Mexico could not live. It is clear from the paintings salvaged from the remains of the priests' houses that there was a considerable philosophy in their religion. A painting of Tlaloc shows him manifesting as the god of the mountains, rising from earth, but it also shows a further manifestation of him within the realm of clouds and beyond into the empyrean, the mysterious world beyond the sphere of the stars. It may well be that much of the theology was cultivated by the use of drugs in a strictly controlled environment. The priests sought for knowledge, and all had their incense-bags always with them as a mark of their profession. No doubt they starved themselves and practised painful austerities as harsh as any of their descendants in Aztec times. Then suddenly the whole thing was destroyed.

What the cause of the destruction of Teotihuacan was is totally unknown to us. There is a gap of over a century between the fall of Teotihuacan and the establishment of the succeeding capital at Tollan where the Toltec lords established themselves. Professor S. Linné, in an excavation at Teotihuacan, found that an early Toltec grave had been dug right through the walls of a ruined and buried building at Teotihuacan. What had happened between the smashing of Teotihuacan and the burial of a Toltec chief on the site of some of its ruins? That we cannot answer. The usual theory is that there was an incursion of more primitive tribes from the north. But although the later Toltecs spoke Nahuat (an old form of the Aztec Nahuatl), which was related to the languages of some of the North American Indians, the real move of Indians from the north came only when the Chichimeca arrived in the eleventh century AD. Nevertheless, a people using a form of the Toltec calendar had long lived on the Pacific coast of Guatemala to the south. Their ceramic styles can be traced earlier to the coasts of San Salvador where they are contemporary with the very founding of Teotihuacan. It is possible that this people had once been affected by the early migration of manioc-growers from the southern shores of the Caribbean sea.

However, the people, who called themselves the Pipiles (princes), built up a high culture and an elaborate near-realist art style when they were settled on the coasts of Guatemala. Their centre was at Santa Lucia Cozumahualpa where several gigantic *stelae* illustrating their religion were erected. Many of these monuments bore inscriptions of day symbols and numbers combined, and all of them can be read as dates in the Toltec-style calendar. At the site of El Castillo one of these remarkable monuments contained a strange picture of the black owl of the planet Venus flying backwards into the rising sun, just as the star Aldebaran was climbing up towards the sun. The dates on the monument proved to be a Venus count, of the days in the phases of the planet. Previously it was thought that this culture dated from the ninth or tenth century AD, but this dated event recorded an actual transit of Venus in December 416 AD.

Thus we have a proto-Toltec inscription carved on the western coast of Guatemala at a date when Teotihuacan was still the great power in Mexico. The transit of Venus took place near sunrise on the coast of Guatemala, so it is possible that the Pipile astronomers actually saw a black spot moving across the face of the sun through the morning mists on the mountains, but it is also possible that they observed it in a mirror of polished obsidian. This was no new invention, for hollow ground magnifying mirrors are known from Olmec times. They could magnify an image quite successfully. But the great point is that the date translated exactly into our calendar and could be correlated exactly with the Aztec calendar dates of ancient times. Thus the Toltec-style calendar was proved to have a continuity from the early fifth century AD.

The sculptured *stelae* from the Cozumahualpa region of Guatemala, many of which are now in Berlin, show us a great deal about the religion of the Pipiles. Human sacrifice was apparently common, and the heart was offered as well as the head. In one case a shrunken, dried human head is shown on the x-shaped cross staff used by Mexican astronomers for their observations. On a famous *stela*, now in Berlin, the planet Venus acquired an alarming form, a great serpent adorned with the symbol of the morning star, extruding from its mouth a figure of a god, presumably Quetzalcoatl, who is offered the heart of a human victim. This is a considerable work of art, but it seems to contradict all we know of the religion of Quetzalcoatl. On other monuments we find skulls and skeletons as symbols of divine power. The dating symbols are shown as a series of rings to

OVERLEAF The Pyramid of the Niches at Tajín, Vera Cruz, probably 10th century AD. This pyramid has 365 niches although there are no figures left in them. There are still Totonac tribes at Tajín.

express numerals, but each ring contains the day-sign associated with it. They mark an early stage in writing dates in the Toltec system and emphasize the importance of the name and deity of the day. But even more importantly the priests and/or nobles are shown in ceremonial dress, rather reminiscent of late Olmec fashion but including the symbolic ornaments of the ball-players which are found in stone in the probably later sculptures of Tajín.

This important series of sculptures from Cozumahualpa is a key statement of the cultural origins of what we know later as the Toltec empire in Mexico. Some curious structures in sculptured figures, especially the incurved shin-bones of standing forms, are found in early Toltec figures, though these latter works are harsh and primitive when contrasted with the greater realism of the Cozumahualpa *stelae* or the delicate decoration of the Totonac versions of similar themes. Yet there is nevertheless a visible stylistic link between the Pipiles of Guatemala, who spoke some form of Nahuat, the peoples of Tajín who overthrew Palenque, and the builders of the Temple of the Feathered Serpents at Xochicalco. Much further study is needed, but it seems as if it was an influence from the Pipiles which led to the violent destruction of the city of Teotihuacan.

The fall of Teotihuacan must have been before 600 AD. It is most probable that, as in later cases, the destruction of the capital city was the cue for the fall of its outlying garrisons. Towns would have been abandoned or fell to local insurrection. Only the cities of the Maya region would have survived untouched. In the Mexican area the Zapotecs continued, and the Teotihuacano artistic influence seems less apparent in later stages while the ceramic styles became somewhat more obviously Zapotec. In the east the Huaxtecs continued in their old ways and produced even more exciting pottery. The Totonacs continued to become more important and reached the highest artistic achievements after the fall of Teotihuacan. Cholula remained a great city, dedicated to its divine Quetzalcoatl. We have no evidence of the usual concomitant of civil war, the eruption of a great pestilence. It is probable but unproven. The great temple pyramids of Teotihuacan remained as centres of pilgrimage. The only place where there was a continuation of Teotihuacano art was the small city of Azcapotzalco. Here art became much more elaborate and rather decadent, but gradually it merges with the arts of the Toltec hegemony.

The general impression one receives of this period before the dawn of true history in Mexico, is one of a destruction of the great city and the emergence of many small city-states with slightly differing cultures. Probably it was an era of intense competition

Stone stele from Santa
Lucia, Cotzumahualpa,
showing a ball-player
saluting the sun, between
6th and 7th centuries AD.

for overlordship. The nature of Mexican civilization was always based on tribal power. The war chief rose more into prominence, apparently after the fall of the theocracy of Teotihuacan. Then war chiefs led their tribespeople into battles to obtain control of the next people. It does not seem to have mattered who was attacked, the whole point was to demonstrate power, to hold tributaries for profit and to obtain captives for the honour of the gods in the great sacrifices. Due to this break-up of unified culture and the so far total lack of historical documents, we find a great lack of continuity. Probably we are seeing an interregnum of almost true tribal anarchy.

It must be admitted, however, that the interregnum after the fall of Teotihuacan saw a level of culture in Mexico infinitely richer than in the period after the disappearance of the Olmec civilizations.

The gap after the Olmec period was one in which much of the artistic skill of the earlier people was lost, though a calendrical system and some of the hierarchy of gods carried on. The level of city building remained low, and any unity seems to have broken up. The cultural gap is apparent even in Oaxaca, where the first sculptures on Monte Alban appear nearly three centuries after the break up of the central Olmec civilization.

Teotihuacan appears to have been an independent development stemming from the agricultural settlements of the valley of Mexico. The whole ambience of the art of the great city was one of religion, and we cannot in Middle America separate religion and war. The gods of Teotihuacan were mainly agricultural, but they carry arms and sometimes appear to act in a warlike manner. Even if the leader of the city was a high priest, there is no reason for assuming that the clerical hierarchy was different from the leaders of the military forces. One finds plenty of traces of heart sacrifice in the paintings and in one at least of the figurines of the city. There can be little doubt that the victims sent to heaven with great ceremony were important warriors taken in battle. One can hardly imagine a Mexican Indian civilization based on agriculture and trade which did not have a strong and active military arm, to protect traders and to enforce the payment of tribute from the outlying regions.

That the imposition of tribute for the enrichment of the central city of Teotihuacan eventually led to the downfall of the regime is possible but not very likely. The main reason for the fall of Middle American cities is normally the ambition of other cities for independence linked with power. The reason for the interregna is the failure of any group to assume responsibility by subverting all their rivals. One may well assume that towards its end the communications between Teotihuacan and the peoples of the isthmus and southwards into Guatemala as far as Kaminaljuyu were cut by developments originating from the Pipiles on the Guatemalan coast and from the Totonacs of the Gulf Coast. This would have cut off the great city from most of its trading advantages and from tributes of rubber, cocoa, tropical feathers etc. It would also stimulate other towns to revolt. But we must be quite clear that none of this has any definite historical recording. No long inscriptions of any kind have come down to us from Teotihuacan, and inscriptions from the Pipiles are all calendrical and have religious rather than historical import. Even the painted histories of Mixtec dynasts do not descend more than a few years into the seventh century A D.

What does Mexico owe to Teotihuacan? Probably the idea of a dominant society holding other tribes in subjection; the full development of a religion of adoration of the powers of nature associated with a complex theology of a three- or four-layered universe; the possibility of survival of a great urban complex surrounding a ceremonial centre. In all these fields Teotihuacan succeeds Olmec ideas to such a degree that the face of civilization was totally changed. A great and truly Mexican Indian civilization was established which would endure for all future generations. In the arts Teotihuacano architects were masters of their craft, but in sculpture there was a tendency to keep figures within the four-square block. In painting and pottery they excelled. They had no metals but managed very well when working in jewel-stones and shell. In all things they remained within the limitations of Middle American technology, with no wheels for transport or for throwing pots and no true arches in construction. From their paintings we deduce that their weavers performed masterly works on the simple back-strap loom. Within these limits they were master craftsmen and creators of beauty.

Pottery animal model, from the River Panuco, northern Vera Cruz, probably 7th century A D or earlier.

3 Toltecs and Aztecs

IN THE LAST CHAPTER THE SITUATION WHICH WAS ANTE-cedent to Toltec civilization was discussed, but it gave no definite information about the true origin of Toltec culture. In later times there was a tradition that the Toltecs had migrated through several places before the founding of their great base at Tollan (Tula, Hidalgo). Perhaps the evidence of the use of the Toltec-style calendar by the Pipiles of Guatemala is the best evidence of their origins. But there is also a strong tradition that they had a northern origin. This may be part of the truth, but the northerners, called Chichimeca by their descendants, were more likely to have invaded Mexico in the eleventh century because of the great drought which set many North American peoples on the move.

It is with the coming of the Toltecs that we find the first extensive use of copper, bronze and gold in Mexico. Their technique was a simple *cire-perdue* casting, which could manage quite complex forms such as hollow-cast cascabels and figurines surrounded by a complex decoration which looks like wire-work. There was much copper ore in north-west Mexico, and there the tribes seem to have developed their own techniques for making weapons and tools. Gold, however, was not so easily found, and it may be that a great deal was imported from Middle America. It was not mined anywhere but obtained from washing river sands.

Toltec social organization was also different from what had gone before. The power was wielded by a military chief who was of equal importance with the high priest and who administered all the civil affairs of the country under his control. This was a militaristic state very different from the earlier divine kingship. The Toltec ruler was entitled the Uei Tlatoani (Great Speaker) because he spoke for all the many tribes under his control. He was also called the Quetzalcoatl, because he was descended directly from the divine Quetzalcoatl, the Morning Star, who was the legendary founder of the dynasty.

It appears that there was a migration and an earlier settlement before the Toltecs founded their major centre. The site of Tollan is

Caryatid figure representing a god with double serpent face mask used as a support for an altar, from Chichen Itza, 11th century AD.

72

a rolling plateau, some twenty miles north of Mexico City. It was from this centre that the nine Toltec Uei Tlatoani spread their rule over the whole of Mexico. The spread appears from their history books to have been irregular, as well as gradual, but by the time of Lord Nine Wind the second, the whole of civilized Mexico had accepted the rule from Tollan.

There has been much debate over the dating of the Toltecs. The traditions of the *Annales de Cuauhtitlán* went back several reigns, but as the names of local chiefs were often repeated, the scientists had to eliminate some of them. The lists were made to fit with the year 1168 when the Aztecs left their homeland, as the year in which Tula fell. Even the lengths of the reigns of Toltec chiefs had been distorted because the great historian of Mexico, Fernando de Alva Ixtlilxochitl, read some of the documents in his possession as indicating that each of the chiefs reigned from a Year One for a period of fifty-two years. But eventually the Vienna Codex (*Codex Vindobonensis, Mexic. 1.*) has yielded a much clearer story.

It contains a series of myths about the creation of the world and leads to the period when the god Quetzalcoatl came to earth to found the Toltec power. The god as described in legend finally sinned with a princess who was a goddess. His excessive use of his huge penis shamed him when he realized his crime, which, however, was committed under the influence of the magic mushroom. He then left Mexico and on a raft of serpent skins sailed towards the sun, which burned up the raft. The heart of Quetzalcoatl ascended into the heavens as the Planet Venus and was seen shining in the sky. The *Codex* shows this event as a solar eclipse in which the sun and planet are both visible. A check with the Royal Observatory at Hurstmonceux showed that the linkage of Venus with a solar eclipse was a rare phenomenon and that this one must have been the eclipse of 16 July 790 AD. At last a definite date for the beginning of truly Toltec rule was established. It is clear from the book that the first Quetzalcoatl was a divine figure. The Toltec scribe was quite convinced that the founder of the ruling line was a god, and that he was Lord of the Morning Star and of the breath of life. There may be a link with the monstrous serpent of the Morning Star shown at Cotzumahualpa a century and a half earlier. But this is not clear. Nevertheless, there can be no doubt that the Toltec version of the Middle American calendar was already present in its fulness at Cozumahualpa.

The *Codex Vindobonensis* shows us that there were nine High Chiefs of the Toltecs. In this it agrees with the Aztec historian Ixtlilxochitl. But whereas he noted that each reign begins with the Year One and thought that it meant that each chief was officially a ruler for fifty-two years, the account in the more ancient codex shows that the average reign was more like twenty years. The fall of Tula must on this evidence be placed at around 980–90 AD.

The *Codex* shows that most but not all of the Toltec rulers extended the area they governed. In the reign of the last but one of the Quetzalcoatls, the empire covered the whole of civilized Mexico. Two of the rulers conducted no outside wars, but instead they celebrated 'Wars of Flowers' in which the warrior societies arranged a mock battle from which each side took enough prisoners to keep the altars of the gods fed with fresh human hearts in the eighteen great festivals of the year. The onward progress of the empire was steady, but suddenly in the reign of the last of the Quetzalcoatl, who was born like his godly ancestor on the day Nine Wind, we find a sudden change. A small group of mountains alone remains of the mighty Toltec Empire. The *Codex* gives no reasons.

Mexican folklore tells us that the god Huitzilopochtli was the cause of the destruction. He was a form of the terrible demi-urge Tezcatlipoca, and he worked magic against the Toltecs. He appeared in the market place of Tollan in the form of a naked Huaxtec trader. The beautiful Princess of Tula went to the market and there saw the trader displaying his handsome naked penis. She was overcome by desire and became ill from her hunger for the man. In the end her father allowed her to marry the stranger. Her child was a son, born on the magical day Nine Wind. He reintroduced the special worship of the war god among the Toltecs and in addition he married a commoner, a beautiful girl but not a member of one of the ruling families. When his father died, the Prince Topiltzin Quetzalcoatl became the High Chief, but most of the local groups of noblemen refused to accept his rule. There was a revolt, and armies from all directions marched and fought until Tollan was destroyed – utterly ruined and desolate. So utterly was it demolished that it was not discovered until the early part of this century, and even then the visible ruins were so meagre that archaeologists thought that they had found a village and that the legends of the greatness of Tula were but a dream.

However, excavation in the last generation has uncovered a desolation of great courtyards and ruined buildings covering some seven square miles. The temples were small when compared to those of Teotihuacan, but the palaces were of great colonnades around courtyards. In the centre of each was a four-square sacrificial mound. So terrible was the destruction of Tollan (now the site of Tula near the village of the same name) that even the temple has been stripped of its sculptured outer stones, and the palaces survive only as high as the walls were covered by the dust

of destroyed walls and burnt timbers. The famous Nine Houses of
Quetzalcoatl were destroyed utterly, but a shell mosaic head of
the god marked the site of what was probably 'The House of
Shells'.

Toltec art was once thought to have been a very magnificent
style, probably because the name Tolteca can mean 'Master
Builder' as well as 'A person from Tollan'. Alas, the art is shown to
be very simple, and what little has survived is rough, or even
crude. However, so thorough has been the destruction of Tollan
that only a few reliefs and walls survive in a sufficiently good
state to tell us of the possibilities of Toltec design. Walls decorated
with frets and cloud scrolls contained layers showing ocelots and
eagles, the symbols of the warrior orders in procession, and there
are rows of serpents holding skulls. All was once brilliantly
coloured. One notes that costume was elaborate, in the normal
Mexican fashion, but that gold had been introduced for personal
ornament. Beads of clay plated with gold have been found, and
fine golden ornaments were worn in the ears. Skirts and leg
ornaments were fringed with copper cascabels, and in some cases
these were made of gold or a gold-copper alloy.

It is probable that the use of gold had come from the Pacific
coast south of Mexico but that its working was then carried on in
Mexico itself. The gold was all placer-mined from river sands.
Copper was smelted, but there was no mining from tunnels. Only
small open-cast areas of ore were worked, and it was similar with
silver, which appears to have been a by-product of the copper
mining. Red cinnabar was heated up to produce mercury, which
was important in forming amalgams with gold and silver in a
simple method of plating. But often gold and copper were melted
together to form an alloy. After this had been cast, the surface was
washed in a strong vegetable acid which removed the copper from
the surface and left a spongy layer of pure gold which was then
burnished. There is no reason to think that the process was a
Mexican discovery. It was identical to processes developed in
Panama and Costa Rica, and rather sadly it never reached the
technical excellence of the more southern artists. However, the
Toltecs were fascinated by the beautiful metal and believed that it
was dropped from the heavens. They called it 'Teocuitlat', which
means the faeces of the gods. Perhaps it would better be translated
as 'Heavenly Droppings'.

Pottery advanced in Toltec times, but they did not discover a
potter's wheel. All vessels were coiled from small rolls of clay. The
best wares were very finely moulded and given a wash of orange
colour. Many were highly burnished by polishing with smooth
pebbles just before firing. Some of the vessels were painted with

Toltec bas relief of a warrior
carrying the head of an
enemy, from Tzompantli at
Chitzen Itza, 12th century
AD. The warrior carries
long-throwing darts and
wears Toltec costume
including, on one arm, a fur
wrap which was used as
a shield.

frescoes of the gods, but they do not survive in any large
numbers. Many rather flat pottery figurines of the deities were
made, and a few of them retain their painting, which shows the
richness of clothing worn by the Toltec ruling classes, their fine
feather ornaments and the great variety of face painting.
Unfortunately the surface of most of the surviving figurines has
lost its paint. However, in Toltec times some potters in southern
Mexico on the borders of eastern Guatemala found a deposit of a
special clay. How they prepared it we do not know, but when a
vessel of grey clay was made, it was painted with a slip of the

finely mixed clay and then fired. The slip turned into a hard and shiny deep green or grey-green colour. This was recognized as an approximation to jade and became very popular. It was traded over the whole of the Toltec Empire. In later times the supplies of the magical clay ran out before the fall of Tollan. Hence the presence of the greenish 'plumbate' wares is a diagnostic of a Toltec date for the deposits in which it is found. 'Plumbate' is a misnomer caused by archaeologists who recognized that the colour was similar to that of lead-glazed wares from Europe. Some modern dealers have discovered that if a piece of plumbate ware is baked at a temperature of about 1200°c, the surface fuses into a true glaze of a beautiful mixture of green and white. But this is not an original method of firing. All Mexican potters baked their ceramics in wood fires which rarely reached a temperature of 950°c.

Alas! We have no surviving examples of Toltec textiles. They are shown as costume in paintings and relief carvings and were obviously rich in design and colour. The women wore wrap-around skirts from waist to mid-calf. Their breasts were covered by a *quechquimitl*, a kind of embroidered poncho with decorated borders. Both skirt and poncho were decorated with fringes around the edges. Sandals were the usual footwear, and anklets and armlets were common dress jewellery. To these were added disc earrings and necklets. Hair was braided and plaited in many different styles, and faces were painted often in yellow with a few red designs stamped on. Men were more decorated than women. Their basic dress was a loincloth and a short skirt. Some wore cloaks or back pendants. The nobles wore broad pendants in the form of stylized birds across their chests, cape-like necklaces, often of jade, with decorated leg-bands and armlets of feather work and enormous head-dresses of shell and feather. The warriors carried soft, flexible shields highly decorated, and on their backs they wore circular discs over their kidneys. These were also areas of splendid decoration in shell and turquoise.

As time went on, the Toltecs became more splendid, and their city of Tollan expanded and became more brilliant. It is clear from the text in *Codex Vindobonensis Mexic. I*, that the empire spread in a series of wars against various other city-states in Mexico until the whole of the civilized area fell into subjection. The series of wars fell into the usual Mexican pattern by which one or another of the cities seized power over others and established an empire based on payment of tribute in return for military protection. It was altogether a militarist organization, but the Toltecs brought in a new form of the more ancient theocratic government, by making a claim to the right to rule the land because the High Chief was a direct descendant of the divine Quetzalcoatl, Lord of the Breath of Life. They were so successful that in all later times Mexican chieftains assumed the right to rule only if they could show some trace of Toltec descent in their ancestry. Thus the cult of Quetzalcoatl remained important, even though in the period of the last Toltec ruler there was a take-over by the power of the god Tezcatlipoca-Huitzilopochtli, the war god, as the principal leader of the pantheon.

The nine High Chiefs of the Toltecs are all recorded in the *Codex Vindobonensis*, but after their ending there appears an undated series of pictures of chiefly figures. Whether they were descendants of the chiefly family or represented the families of survivors of the *débâcle* in Mexico, remains uncertain. But on the back of the *Codex* another artist has painted a list of the Mixtec Indian Lords of Tilantongo. The chiefs are all known from other Mixtec codices, and it is clear that the *Vindobonensis* list ends soon after 1350 AD. As the last Chiefs were listed, the scribe had succumbed to a sense of urgency and he has omitted the figures and written just the names of the last rulers. It is possible that the date about 1350 represented some terrible defeat of the Mixtecs, and it may explain how it came into the hands of the Aztecs. It is certain that the *Codex* was in Europe before the final end of the Aztec power, so it is reasonably certain that it was sent by the great Emperor Montezuma II to Hernando Cortes, whom he believed to be the returned Toltec god Quetzalcoatl.

The end of the Toltec rule over Mexico was a very terrible event. Not only was the capital, Tollan, thoroughly desecrated and destroyed but the war spread over the whole of Mexico. The stories of the time tell us of a great plague caused by the rotting bodies of warriors in the fields. It is said that only seven Toltec noble families remained in the country. There was an almost total eclipse of civilization, but some towns survived and some of them were controlled by families of Toltec descent who by their lights had the right to rule over their neighbours. Whatever the meaning of this right, it certainly led to many noble families from other regions trying to marry the heiresses of these families so that some vestige of Toltec magic should fall upon their children, giving them the 'divine right' to rule.

Now that the kingly dates in the *Vienna Codex* have become available to us, the whole picture of the period after the fall of Tollan becomes more clear. We are dealing with the eleventh century AD. The crash of the empire was paralleled in North America by a terrible period of drought. There are myths and tales about this as the period when the Mississippi dried up. Archaeologically this is the period when the Pueblo Indians were driven

A page from a Mixtec codex, showing domestic marriages, including that of the 11th-century chief Eight-Deer Ocelot Claw, who is offered a vase of cocoa by his wife: *Codex Zouche-Nuttall*, now in the British Museum, 14th century AD.

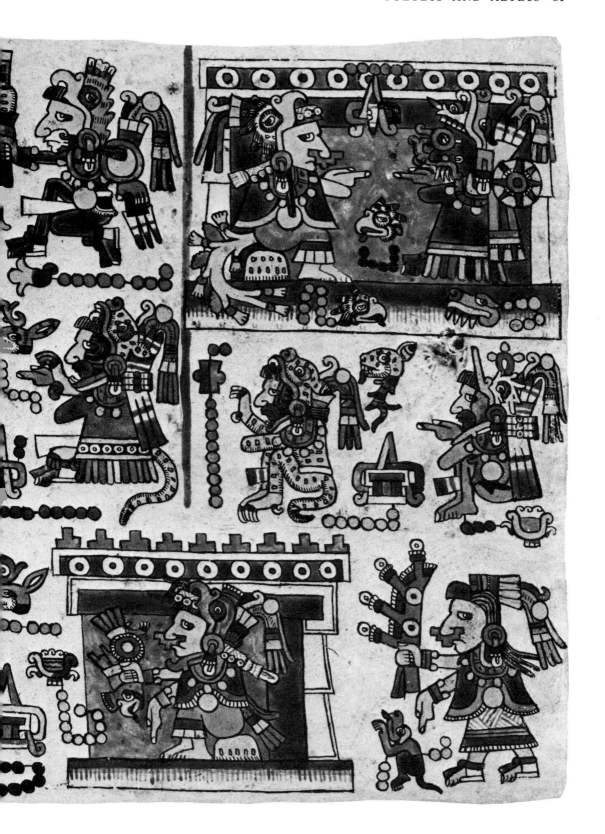

to build settlements in caves. So we have an explanation of the coming of the Chichimeca. Their name means 'Those who go chi-chi-chi when they speak'. In other words, they were foreign migrants speaking an incomprehensible tongue.

There are long stories of how the great Chichimec chief Xolotl organized his tribes and founded city states. It is probable that the invasions were caused by drought, and blessed with prosperity when the power of the Toltecs was no longer there to afford protection. So, many tribes entered Mexico. A story tells of how Xolotl came to the tragic burnt remains of Tollan and wept over the destruction. In those days not a building had been left standing. The past tragedy remained all too evident. But the infusion of new Chichimec blood into Mexico was a stimulus and improved the cultural level of that world once more. Chichimec became a term of honour, referring back to brave chieftains and great conquerors. The Chichimec absorbed Mexico, but they did not form any empire. They became the rulers of independent and often very ancient cities. Tezcoco on the shores of the Lake of Mexico was one of them. It may possibly be that the Aztecs were one of their groups, since it is clear that an early Aztec chief adjusted tribal history to suit the newly found grandeur of his people.

It is interesting to note that the Aztec account of twelfth-century events almost exactly reproduces a Mixtec account of events nearly two centuries earlier, immediately after the fall of Tollan. The original is recorded in the Mixtec document the *Selden Roll* in the Bodleian Library in Oxford.

It seems that the Mixtecs (their name means Cloud people, because they lived high in the mountains of Mexico) were an important constituent of the Toltec hegemony. The most splendid of their history books, *Codex Zouche-Nuttall* in the British Museum, records their emergence in the sixth century AD from a sacred tree at Apoala. Later on, we find that a great Mixtec chief, the Lord Smoking Eyes, married a Lady Three-stone-knife in the great city of Tollan. It appears that they believed their chief to be descended from the planet Venus. One wonders whether this implied that he was a High Chief of the Toltecs? But three generations later, we find another noble wedding celebrated in the blackened ruins of a city, marked by its reed symbol as Tollan.

Somewhat later we find the records of the Mixtec Chief Eight Deer, Ocelot Claw, Lord of the town of Tilantongo (Place of Black Earth). Eight Deer, born in the year 1002, died as a self-dedicated sacrifice in 1054. His remarkable story is painted in detail on the verso side of the *Codex*. He was a minor princeling who, with his brother, offered a sacrifice to the sun god who descended from the

sky to accept it. He was apparently dedicated to the god
henceforward. After some internal fighting, Eight Deer organized
a military force and proceeded to capture many mountain towns.
We are given lists of these small towns and their chiefs and later
shown that he descended from the mountains to capture towns in
the Zapotec region of Oaxaca. Eventually he captured the High
Chief of the Zapotecs, but since this man was also a god, he was
treated with great respect, though he still had to pay tribute.

Finally after several other adventures the Lord Eight Deer,
Ocelot Claw, sacrificed his brother, who had been present at the
vision of the sun-god. Two years later he had his own heart
offered to the god.

This history, painted in the most beautiful of all the surviving
codices (it too was completed in about 1350), gives a good idea of
the general aspect of struggle during the interregnum between the
fall of Tollan and the rise of the Aztec city Tenochtitlan. There
were several small groupings of towns around a major city. The
Zapotecs ruled from Mitla once the Mixtecs' army had left their
country. In the east the Huaxtecs and Totonacs continued their
local rule. The great holy city of Cholula remained independent,
as a centre of learning for some centuries. Many another city was
independent and reasonably powerful. All worshipped the same
pantheon of gods, and all conducted wars so that human victims
could honourably be captured for sacrifice to the gods. In many of
the towns power was exercised by chiefs of Chichimec origin,
who by marriage had acquired descent from the ancient Quetzalcoatls of the Toltecs. Few had a long history, for any war might
end in the destruction of tribal records. One in particular kept its
annals, the small town of Cuauhtitlan (At the Place of the Eagle)
which recorded local and area chiefs right back through time to
the rulers of Tollan. The records counted back year by year, and
though the earlier parts are very sketchy, there was a link.
Unfortunately many names of chiefs were repeated more than
twice, and learned historians decided that they were repetitions
of the same person so that the list should fit to a theoretical date of
1168 for the fall of Tollan (now the site of Tula). This was a little
more than three calendar-rounds of fifty-two years in their
system, in error. But those scant annals do form a bridge over the
years from the fall of a great empire to the rise and development of
Aztec power.

The story of the Aztecs begins according to their official
version, in a town of the Crane (Aztatlan), later called Aztlan.
There the ancestors decided to leave, as instructed by an oracle of
their god Huitzilopochtli (Humming-bird on the Left, a symbol of
the sun). They gathered around a tree and ate some of the

forbidden fruit, which angered their god, and they were
condemned to wander around the land, settling a few years here
and a few more there, until they were totally defeated and
enslaved by the Lord of Culhuacan. It may well be that in truth
they moved into Mexico from an area of California, but that awaits
proof. However, the enslaved people were a nuisance, as recorded
in *Codex Boturini*. Coxcoxtli, Lord of Culhuacan sent them out to
fight a superior enemy. They carried the image of their god with
them, laid an ambush and seized the enemy army. They killed
every man for their god and cut off the left ear of each corpse.
Then, apparently empty handed, they returned to Culhuacan.
When upbraided for being cowards and avoiding the enemy, they
opened their packs and poured hundreds of human ears over the
feet of Coxcoxtli.

The chief was horrified and sent the Aztecs away to a group of
rocks and swampy islets in the Lake. There the poor Aztecs saw a
stream of red and blue water, the symbol for war, and then they
came to a rock on which there grew a great cactus. Sitting on the
cactus was their god in the form of a white sea-eagle. He held a
serpent in his talons, and they knew that this was to be their
permanent home and that they should eventually conquer all the
lands between the seas. So they built a small temple, installed the
sacred image and made sacrifices.

The second Aztec chief captured a small town on the mainland;
the third married a princess of true Toltec descent and captured
and destroyed Culhuacan. A battle was fought for control of the
spring of fresh water from Chapultepec Hill which still supplies
good drinking-water to Mexico City. From that point there was no
going back. The Aztec people were a tribal power to be reckoned
with by the neighbouring towns. They had acquired the Toltec
right to rule through two judicious marriages. They were still
something of a Plains Indian type of democracy in that the chiefs
were elected by the whole community, but that was to change.

The city had to face a planned attack by several neighbouring
states led by Azcapotzalco. The mass of the people feared that
they would be defeated by what seemed to be an immensely
superior force. But there were still those among them who
remembered the ancient days of enslavement. The leaders of three
of the most noble families called a conference, and the people
debated the whole question. There was no doubt that they were
in a position of great danger. The chieftains suggested that
resistance was the only way, that their war god had promised that
once they were established in Cactus Rock, as they were now,
they should rule the whole land between the seas. In the end, they
came to an arrangement that the nobles would lead the battle and

Aztec squatting ocelot in stone, probably a symbol of the ocelot warrior society, 16th century AD.

that all the people would accept the consequences. If they were defeated, they would offer the rulers as a peace offering. But if they won, they would agree that for ever more they would elect the supreme chiefs from one of the noble families. The young warriors went out in the darkness and laid their ambushes in the cornfields and woodlands so recently acquired for the Aztecs. They knew that the enemy would attempt to cut off the supply of fresh water from Chapultepec, and so they knew where the main attack would come. As the sun rose, both sides offered sacrifices, and captives were slain in honour of the tribal gods. The Ocelot warriors were ready and moved silently among the rocks; then, as the enemy advanced, they moved around and slipped to his rear. The army moved down to the shores of the Lake, then the attack came from flanks and rear. The war shouts and whistles called out, arrows flew and the war darts cast from throwing sticks pierced many a shield and cut down warriors. Others were captured by young braves carrying ropes and nets in which they dragged captives away for sacrifice. Then, as confusion reigned, the main body of the Aztecs, the Eagle warriors, attacked from the lake shore. They surged forward and made an area of land into a pen in which the enemy were systematically massacred or captured. The battle ended in a total Aztec victory. For ever afterwards the cities on the northern shores of the lake would pay tribute to the Aztec rulers of Tenochtitlan.

Great numbers of captives were taken to the top of the temple and sacrificed to the gods. The people ate many small pieces of human flesh cut from the limbs of the victims. The war god was satisfied, and the people were happy. Nevertheless, the establishment of the Aztec power was but the beginning of a continuous process. The great war chief Itzcoatl (Serpent of sharp stones), who reigned until 1440 as a great and dangerous warrior, seems to have been the man who had all the ancient records destroyed and who reconstructed the past story of his people. His basic story of origins seems to have been taken from sources of Toltec origin, for it is clearly painted in many of the Mixtec stories which tell of their contact with the Toltecs. The important part was the legend of a tribal homeland known as the Chicomoztoc, the Seven Caves. From this the peoples of central Mexico had migrated one after another, the last being the ancestors of the Aztecs. The documents go on to describe how the dark forces had introduced mankind to the necessity of human sacrifice. In the face of all archaeological evidence, one of the Mixtec versions puts this event in the tenth to eleventh century AD, and the Aztec official story puts the same series of revelations in the late twelfth century. The migrant tribes saw mutilated victims laid out on cactus plants. Their god told them that the victims must be sacrificed by the removal of their hearts and then led them on their migration which resulted in victory. One can only assume that the legend was already ancient and sacred, and that Itzcoatl simply fitted his tribal history into the accepted pattern. The Aztecs became one with the rest of the population of the Valley of Mexico. They would no longer be regarded as a lesser or even as a foreign people.

However, the Aztecs had friendly contacts among the lakeside tribes. They had been assisted by the people of the little city of Tlacopan and formed an alliance with them. Then the great and powerful city of Tezcoco had been friendly. The Tezcocan chiefs traced their descent to the great Chichimec leader Xolotl, who had wept among the ruins of Tollan. They had established themselves as the most enlightened and intelligent of the rulers in central Mexico. For a long time they had been in friendly contact with the Mexicans, especially under their wise chief Hungry Coyote (Nezahualcoyotl), who had been driven into exile by a distant cousin who had seized power. The Aztec tribe organized to work around Tezcoco and attack it in conjunction with a rising of the supporters of Hungry Coyote, who had won his name through his sufferings as an exile. The attack was successful, and then Tezcocans proposed a triple alliance of Tezcoco, Tenochtitlan and Tlacopan. This alliance lasted through the succeeding couple of centuries until the coming of the Spaniards. As time went on, the balance altered, and the Aztecs became the dominant partner, but when the triple Alliance was concluded, the Tezcocans expected that they would be the leaders. However, the Aztecs relied on the promise of their god. Itzcoatl took his armies around the whole of the Lake of Mexico, capturing many small towns and in particular seizing Xochimilco, the Field of Flowers, still the flower-garden of Mexico City. Thus he became a very great war leader and assumed the title of Uei Tlatoani, which implied leadership of many peoples. It can be roughly translated as Emperor.

In 1440 Itzcoatl died, and his war leader Moctecuzomatzin Ilhuicamina (Strong Arm who Shoots at the Heavens) or to us Montezuma I, succeeded him. He was a man of civilization and brought the waters of Chapultepec into his island city by means of a great aqueduct, which still functions today.

The range of wars and plundering raids made by the allies spread mostly to the west and south. The altars of Mexico City and Texcoco were always bloody with the fruits of human sacrifice. But the glory of the Aztecs was enhanced. The other tribes dreaded them but paid tribute or lived in fear of the day when they would be conquered. However, Montezuma revived the Toltec custom of the War of Flowers, so that prisoners might

Aztec stone carving of [the] Hungry Coyote, possibly in memory of Nezahualcoyotl, Lord of Tezcoco, early 16th century AD.

be taken in a kind of tournament battle even when there was no political war on hand. Thus the gods were always sure of their food and the honours of worship. The sun continued his course in the sky, nourished by the human blood poured out for him so lavishly.

Montezuma I was succeeded in 1469 by the chief Axayacatl (Face of Water). In his days the town of Tlaltelolco, which shared the same island as the Aztec capital, started a war. Its chief Moquiuhix was a coward and when defeated committed suicide by leaping from the top of his temple pyramid. This was so disgraceful that the body was left to rot in the place made unhallowed by such a suicide. Tlatelolco then became, as it is now, part of Mexico City. The main contribution of Axayacatl to Mexican art was his command that a great slab of porphyry should be carved with the symbols of the sun and the passage of time. It was erected about half way up the great temple staircase and can be used by mathematicians for calculating eclipses of the sun both forward and backward in time. In his reign the Aztec armies captured the isthmus of Tehuantepec. They also tried to break out to the north-west but were terribly defeated by a Tarascan army and never went that way again. It appears that they felt that their god was driving them in another direction towards the conquests which would make them rulers of the lands between the seas.

Tizoctzin came to power in 1479, a pusillanimous chief detested by his army commanders. There were but few and minor conquests in his reign, though he had an enormous circular stone made for sacrificial combats. The carvings around the edge of the stone represent Tizoc dressed as the Aztec war god, capturing chiefs of different towns and dragging them off by their hair to sacrifice. But, alas, most of these records are copied from conquests made by his late brother. However, he did commence the work of rebuilding the great temple. The method was, as before, to cover the existing temple pyramid with a fine new coating which made it larger than before. This work had reached half way before the reign of Tizoc came to a sudden end in 1486. Some say that the Aztec war leaders had conspired to have the unlucky Emperor murdered.

Tizoc was succeeded by a splendid and luxury-loving leader of the nation, the Water Beast, Ahuitzotl. It was said that he had all the most beautiful women as junior wives, and that his love of music made the city always resound with the songs coming from his palace. He brought much more gold into the city and decorated many splendid buildings. But his great work was the completion of the temple of the war god and of the rain spirit. He pushed on the work and imported stone-carvers from Malinalco to make the splendid decorations. Then, to express the glory and power of his people, he made a war into the mountains of Oaxaca. There he took the whole man-power of three Mixtec tribes. Twenty thousand men were brought into Mexico, bound and plastered with white eagle-down stuck on them by their own blood. They were all slain on the pyramid. The high chiefs of the Aztecs and the Tezcocans killed the first ones, and then the priests took over, slashing the chests of the victims and passing the hearts to be smeared on the faces of the idols. So many were slain that the people could not eat the flesh from the limbs, and half the bodies were thrown into the marshes. Mexico was shocked. Nezahualpilli, Lord of Tezcoco, protested at the horrors, but to no avail. It had been necessary to sacrifice only twenty warriors for the dedication, but the Aztecs insisted on their twenty thousand victims. It was partly a self-glorifying act of propaganda to spread fear of their name over all the tribes. Instead it aroused a deep-seated complex of fear compounded with hatred which was to be the root cause of the destruction of Aztec power. It was, however during the reign of Ahuitzotl that the promise of the war god was fulfilled, for the Aztec armies overcame the Huaxtecs and so reached the Atlantic coast. Thus their power was at last reaching from sea to sea. Their land was in very truth Anahuac, 'between the waters'. In other directions the armies had entered Guatemala and had finally subverted the great city of Cholula, the sacred centre of Quetzalcoatl. Only the Tlaxcalans remained free, but that was because these warlike mountain folk were considered useful as a reservoir of sacrificial victims in case there was no one else to fight.

Ahuitzotl's death was sudden. There had been a disastrous flood due to some volcanic upheaval which had sent the waters of the Lake boiling over and destroyed great sections of the protective wall. The men of Tezcoco came over to join the Aztecs in the repair works, and Ahuitzotl went to visit the site. He went on the wall, his foot slipped and he fell, cutting his head. In three days the great war leader was no more. The tribal Council met and selected his nephew Moctecuzoma Xocoyotzin (Mighty Lord, He of the Strong Arm) to be his successor as Speaker of the Peoples. This great ruler was a slender, golden skinned young man with a slight beard. He was a little over thirty years of age and had already distinguished himself as a war leader. So in 1503, when, unbeknown to the Aztecs, there were already Spanish colonies in the West Indian islands, Montezuma II came to rule. He made successful raids to capture prisoners for his accession ceremonies. Soon came a very important date, the year 1507, which in the

The dedication stone of the great temple at Tenochtitlan, carved in 1487, and representing the Aztec war chiefs Tizoc and Ahuitzotl offering their blood in the year 8 Acatl (1487).

Aztec jade figure of Xolotl,
Lord of the Evening Star,
16th century AD.

Aztec calendar was the beginning of a round of fifty-two years. Great ceremonies were held, the New Fire was made and amid hopeful rejoicings the Aztecs entered on another step in their history. Nobody knew it was to be their last, though Montezuma had a foreboding of coming perils.

The next year, 1508, saw a transit of the planet Venus across the face of the sun. No doubt the astrologers prophesied and Montezuma paid special attention because Venus was, as morning star, the symbol of Quetzalcoatl, who was not only an ancestor of Montezuma but was also born on the same calendrical day, Nine Wind. So the great ruler had a figure of Quetzalcoatl carved wearing the sun as a necklace. It was made from a forty-pound boulder of jade and is now in the Museum of Mankind in London.

However, the life of Montezuma was chequered: there were victories and further conquests along the coast, but there were also defeats, and the people suffered from famine. As time went on, the strange events became more frequent. A flame was seen in the sky, lasting for most of the night and persisting for some years. People saw the spirits of the dead weeping for some future disaster, and Montezuma's aunt visited the land of the dead and returned after four days of trance in which she had seen the destruction of the great city of Cactus Rock and the death of Montezuma. The strange apparitions were due partly to the Mexican belief in magic and partly to the reports of strange ships visiting the coasts.

Then came Hernando Cortes. He landed on the day on which it was possible that the god Quetzalcoatl would return to claim victory over the war god of the Mexicans. He wore a costume which strongly recalled the dress which the god was said to wear. This all fitted in with the expectations of Montezuma. He sent to Cortes a mass of treasure, some masks of the gods, much gold and a group of books which included the ancient book of Quetzalcoatl, now in Vienna. The stranger accepted the gifts with becoming courtesy, mostly because he was instructed by a teenage Mexican girl Ce Malinalli, who was destined to destroy the Aztec power. She knew it, and even though she became Cortes's mistress, she pursued her destiny with a great determination and considerable kindness.

Montezuma could not understand why the god was busy advising the conquered Totonac Indians to revolt. But they did revolt, and Montezuma was unable to punish them. He tried out many magical devices to test the authenticity of Cortes-Quetzalcoatl, but Doña Marina (as the Spaniards called Ce Malinalli) was able to circumvent them. So the tensions remained and Montezuma was driven into a state of misery in which he

Carved stone vase, possibly Mixtec work, presented to Cortes by Montezuma in 1519. The front (*left*) represents the dead sun of the jaws of the earth, and the
back (*opposite*) shows the Sun diving from a day-symbol Olin, which will eventually mark the end of creation.

Mixtec gold and turquoise pendant, about 3 inches in diameter, representing the shield and war darts of an army commander, from Monte Alban, 13th century AD.

found it impossible to command his people to attack the enemy. His problem was that as a man he was dedicated to Quetzalcoatl by the date of his birth, but as High Chief of the Aztecs he was dedicated to Huitzilopochtli, a form of the dreadful Tezcatlipoca who was the deadly foe to Quetzalcoatl. Thus the ruler was torn in two ways. He remembered the conflict which had destroyed his ancestors, the Toltec rulers. He had a small house among the ruins of Tollan, and he went there to consider the future but could not rest. He was sure the newcomers would win, but he was also sure that he must try to defend the Aztecs to the last.

Little by little the iron-clad Spaniards, proof against the Aztec weapons of wood and stone, advanced. They captured Tlaxcala, destroyed a Mexican army at Cholula and eventually appeared in Mexico. They were astonished at the beauty of the capital, larger than any city of Europe in those days. The great pyramid temples rose in its heart, and they well knew the meaning of the red stains flowing down the steps from the god-houses on top. Then they rode over the causeways leading across the lake. There they met Montezuma, carried in a golden palanquin. He walked on fine cloth, which was spread before him because he was so sacred that

Aztec war drum with relief of the Sun God as Huitzilopochtli, Lord of War, from Toluca, 15th century AD. The middle band has the symbols of shields floating on the war waters and the lower part has symbols of the ocelot warrior society.

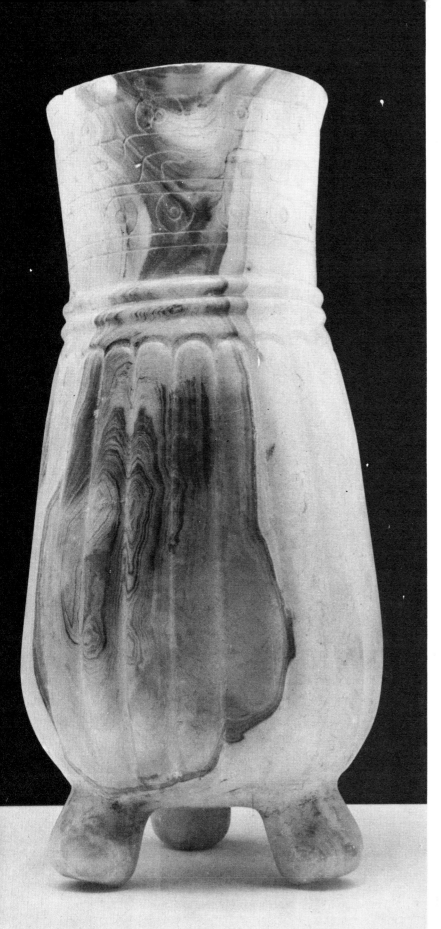

Aztec carved calcite vase
for cacao, 16th century A D.

Mixtec tripod vase with serpent's feet and painted symbol of a diving fire-serpent, from Oaxaca, between 14th and 15th centuries AD.

his feet must not touch the ground. He was covered in gold and turquoise, and his nobles wore great quantities of gold with their fine cloth cloaks and feathered headdresses. The welcome was kindly, though the Spaniards sensed their danger.

Their stay in the palaces of the city was quite a long one, but they seized Montezuma and made him a hostage. Then they demanded gold and more gold. But one day they heard that another Spanish army had landed in order to arrest Cortes. The latter left Mexico City and put his warrior friend Alvarado in charge of the garrison. The main part of the army went to the coast and defeated their rivals. Many of the new soldiers joined them and marched back to Mexico. When they returned, the city was silent. It seemed full of menace. Cortes found out that Alvarado had been scared by a great parade of Mexican war chiefs

Mixtec golden pendant representing the Sun Eagle descending on a butterfly, from Monte Alban, Oaxaca, 12th or 13th century AD.

Gigantic Aztec stone statue of the Earth Goddess Coatlicue ('Serpent Lady'), early 16th century AD. It was excavated in 1819 from the great temple site in Mexico City.

in honour of their gods. The Spaniards had cut them to pieces and so aroused national resentment. They knew that trouble was coming. Soon they were besieged in the palace where they held Montezuma a prisoner. They took him up to the walls to calm his people, but a sling stone struck him down. His heart was broken by the revolt and within a week he died, refusing to speak to his captors. They gave his body to the Mexicans, who cremated it. But the danger was so great that the Spaniards decided to slip out of the city on the first moonless night. As they crossed the causeway, they were seen. A terrible fight took place, and two thirds of the Spanish force were slain before they reached the mainland.

The remainder of the army with Cortes retreated into mountainous Tlaxcala. The Aztecs did not harass them very much. Their new ruler Cuitlahuac was ill with the smallpox which had been introduced into Mexico by a soldier in the army of invaders which Cortes had defeated. Cuitlahuac died and was succeeded by the brave nineteen-year-old Falling Eagle, Cuauhtemoc. Then the battles recommenced. Eventually the Spanish and Tlaxcalan forces surrounded the lake and blockaded Mexico. They advanced, fighting, across the causeways. The Aztecs refused to surrender, then Cortes had to destroy the beautiful city house by house until he reached the central square. There one of his boats brought in a prisoner, the brave Cuauhtemoc, last ruler of Aztec Mexico. The date was 21 August 1521.

The fall of Tenochtitlan (Cactus Rock), as Mexico City used to be known, was a terrible disaster. The ruins of the town were deserted for half a year so that the thousands of corpses could rot without poisoning the people. Then gangs went back to level out the ruins and prepare the way for the splendid new Spanish city of Mexico. In the interval the Spanish soldiers were sent far and wide throughout the country to seize all gold and silver. It is a grim story of cruelty and rapine. Hundreds of tons of precious metal were seized. The Spaniards were apparently incapable of recognizing the work as having any artistic value. All was melted down in the interests of equality. The Royal Fifth was sent to Spain in ingot form, and the leaders among the *conquistadores* each took their agreed share in metal ingots.

The Spaniards had little use for golden chains and bracelets. They did not wear bells in their noses, nor did masks of the heathen gods decorate earrings for them. Cortes tried hard to help the native population which he had seized. But he followed the Spanish pattern established in dealing with the Moors in the homeland. Great bodies of Indians were given in *repartimientos* to Spanish landowners who were enjoined to treat them well and teach them the rudiments of Christianity. In some cases the masters were wise and kindly men, but in many the condition of the Indians was reduced to a cruel slavery. The Church tried to preach to the landowners, but the friars were tricked or driven away to their convents. But the upper-class Indians, the descendants of the Toltec Lords of Mexico, were regarded as being equivalent to Spanish Grandees and retained positions of authority and power. It is to their writings that we owe much of our knowledge of Aztec life. But above all others we are indebted to Father Bernardino de Sahagún, a Franciscan priest who came to Mexico in 1545. He taught at the old church and convent in Tlaltelolco, which still stands beside modern workers' flats and the ruins of ancient temples. There he wrote a great book, *The Things of New Spain*, which was compiled from the answers given to his questions by his pupils, who questioned their parents and grandparents about the Aztec way of life before the Spaniards came. The Inquisition forbade the publication of his book for over fifty years, but he wrote it once in the Aztec language, Nahuatl, and then added a Spanish translation. He used native artists to illustrate the work with a series of small vignettes which give a true picture of life in ancient Mexico.

In the book of Father Sahagún we can learn of the practice of healing by herbs, of how to estimate fortunes from the dates of the native Calendar, of making of food and brewing of drink. All Mexican life is there.

The section of Father Sahagún's book on the work of the goldsmiths is a revelation of the simplicity of the craft, and indeed it makes us wonder all the more about the consummate skill of the goldsmiths. The raw metal was placer-washed from the sands in stream beds. There was little mining, though the silver workers dug their ore from rock faces, and sometimes with the black rock from which the silver was extracted they found grains and small nuggets of gold. They also dug into the rocks for the greenish stones from which copper could be melted and the black stones which produced tin. In the case of gold the grains of metal were heated in a crucible over a fire of charcoal. A group of young apprentices sat around the fire blowing through copper tubes to increase the heat, for no one in Mexico had discovered the use of bellows. When the metal was molten, it was poured in a thin layer onto a smoothed stone plate so that it set as a thin flat ingot ready for further use.

Next the goldsmith prepared the core for his finished work. It was modelled in a mixture of clay and charcoal to be as exactly as possible the shape of the finished product. After two days it was dry, and the craftsman took thin layers of beeswax softened with

Mosaic mask based on a human skull. This probably represents Tezcatlipoca in his form of Itzcoliuhqui, Lord of Darkness, 15th century AD. It was presented to Cortes by Montezuma.

Santa Cecilia – the only
Aztec temple to survive
the Spanish conquest.

a little oil. This he laid on the core and worked up exactly with tiny tools so that precisely every part of the golden object would be modelled. Raised parts were applied to the surface in the form of tiny vermicelli-like rolls of wax. Then all was left to dry for another two days. Next the wax model and core were prepared for the casting; a broad wax rod was made to leave a space for the gold to be poured in, and several smaller rods were added at strategic points to allow the gases to escape without damaging the casting. Then the whole was painted over with a fine paste of charcoal powder, which was backed by a coarser paste of charcoal and clay. Again two days were taken for drying. Then the apprentices prepared two fires of charcoal which they proceeded to blow to white heat through their pipes. When the wax model melted and poured out of its mould while burning, so that it left an empty space to be filled with gold, the mould was heated still further, little by little so that it did not crack. Meanwhile, a small crucible rather like a ladle was heated with a sufficiently large piece of gold. When it was evenly melted, the metal was poured into the spout of the mould. Any remaining wax hissed out of the small blow holes. The master goldsmith shook his work or even swung it round while still white hot so that the metal should fill every space, and then it was gently laid on the hot charcoal to cool down slowly. The next step was to break away the mould and dig out the clay core. The golden object was then seen. If there were any gaps, they were filled with a little melted gold. Then the whole thing was boiled in water with alum to clean the surface. Finally it was burnished smooth and brilliant with tools made from hard agate. Then the lovely object, after a week's work, was ready to be worn.

In this way they made bells and pendant birds' heads with movable tongues, little figures of animals with jointed limbs and many another treasure, few of which remain. The finest collection known was excavated by the late Dr Alfonso Caso on Monte Alban in Oaxaca. It comprised a set of personal jewels belonging to a Mixtec chief buried there in the thirteenth century.

The size of golden objects varied: perhaps the largest was a great disc of gold which was the stretch of a man's arms wide. It was modelled all over with symbols and had been hidden in the water weeds of a pond in the gardens of Guauhtemoc's palace. The Spaniards thought it was beautiful and would not at first break it up. So the young soldier who found it gambled with a friend and lost the sun in a night's play. But as Cortes had to send the Royal Fifth as tribute to the King of Spain, the glorious sun symbol had to be melted down and the ingots weighed out before the fifth was sent off to Europe.

Aztec seated figure of the Death Goddess Mictlanciuhatl, 16th century AD. She is wearing a feathered dancing skirt with shell rattles as a fringe.

Most of the splendid buildings of old Tenochtitlan were destroyed in the final battle, but the vast body of the great pyramid survived another generation. But then it was blown up by five hundred barrels of gunpowder. Fortunately the Mexican houses built by the Spaniards needed no glass in their windows. The ruins were levelled, and there in the great square of Mexico City, the Zocalo is marked by the Cathedral, around the back of which can be seen a few ruined walls of parts of the ancient temple which had been preserved because they were buried under the debris. In 1819 the English traveller William Bullock noticed that every November the Aztecs came to the square and placed heaps of marigolds upon one spot. He had the place dug over and there came up a gigantic statue of the Earth Goddess; she was terrifyingly ugly to the white man, but the Indians still loved their dear Mother Earth. She now stands majestically in the heart of the great Museum of Anthropology, amid figures of other gods and the treasures of Mexico's past.

Only a little of the featherwork from ancient Aztec times survives. In Vienna one may see a beautiful feather fan with a butterfly design, the great Quetzal-feather head-dress which Montezuma wore when acting for the War God and the featherwork shield of his predecessor the High Chief Ahuitzotl. In Stuttgart there is a shield of an army commander and another shield of a great chief, and in Berlin, until the end of World War II, there was a strange black and white feather hanging, perhaps from an image of the death god, but this has disappeared. There is always hope that it may turn up again from some forgotten hiding-place.

Of the books of ancient Mexico, there are most in Britain. The Bodleian Library in Oxford houses four, the British Museum two, and at Liverpool is another one. In Europe there are two in Paris and two in Vienna, three in Berlin, one in Bologna and none in Spain. But in Spain there are two of the best of the magical books of the Maya who form the subject of our next chapter.

4 The Maya Cities

THE MAYA HOMELAND IS TO THE SOUTH OF MEXICO. IT covered the whole of the Yucatan peninsula, parts of Guatemala right into the Cordillera, some of Nicaragua and most of Honduras and San Salvador. There are no migration legends. The Maya believed that they represented a fourth attempt of their gods to people the earth. Apparently they had no history, or else we have no key to discover it. Where history is found, it takes the shape of the books of Chilan Balam which are of eleventh- or twelfth-century origins and were made after the Toltecs had assumed control over the greater part of the people.

In the field of prehistory we find that the oldest dated monuments go back only to the first century AD. But archaeology shows that pottery styles and architecture of distinctively Maya style go back for another two or three centuries. Earlier than this we find that simpler pottery forms and small buildings mark village sites which may have been Maya back to times when the Olmecs were important on the southern coast of the country. There must have been some connection because Maya architecture stems from an Olmec base, and Maya writing shows some echoes of Olmec design.

Our clues to the nature of Maya writing come from the work of a sixteenth-century missionary bishop, Diego de Landa, who wrote a long account of Maya life in his book *The Things of Yucatan*. But unfortunately he was misled into thinking that there was a Maya alphabet. In fact the Maya, alone of all the American Indian peoples may have used phonetic writing, with a syllabary of about 650 characters. Fortunately Landa's account of the calendrical system was correct, and we can now read Maya dates with considerable accuracy. Among the slight variations of the accepted scheme which vary by only about three days, the exact one is that propounded by Martinez, but it is complicated by the fact that the Maya reckoned their day from sunset, and so an evening date is counted as tomorrow. However, the system is sufficiently clear for us to follow the calculations and to date accurately any monument with a calendar inscription.

Late Maya figure of Kukulcan wearing his wind jewel, from Yucatan, probably 14th century AD.

107

Relief sculpture from Yaxchilan showing a heavily jewelled priest wearing a god mask and feathered headdress, c. 8th or 9th century AD.

Maya bas relief figure of a priest holding a castanet, from Palenque, 7th century AD. Note the curious deformation of his skull.

While the basic calendar of the Maya was precisely similar to that of other Middle American peoples, except that they named days in their own language, they extended their time count in multiples of twenty, e.g. 20 × 18 days was a *tun*; 360 days × 20 = a *Katun*. 360 × 20 × 20 = a *Baktun*. And so on. If the local priests needed to calculate back, they were capable of working in periods of many millions of tuns. But whatever calculation they made, they always added a supplementary series of dates to bring their final date into line with the position of the sun at an exact number of solar years. Their count of 360 day *tuns* was always short of the $365\frac{1}{4}$ day year. The accuracy of the time-counting of the Maya is excellent. Their calculation of the true length of the solar year was slightly better than ours.

The word *tun* means a stone. When twenty of these 'stones' had accumulated, every Maya town erected a great stone monument in honour of the presiding deity of the coming period of twenty *tuns* (105 days short of twenty years). Sometimes these time markers are flat slabs of limestone, some six feet in height, and sometimes they are great monolithic blocks twenty feet high. All of them are adorned with heroic figures, apparently of one or other of the four Bacabs, the gods who hold up the corners of the sky. Each figure is shown holding a ceremonial bar across its chest, usually in the form of a double-headed serpent, which represents the heavens. Usually they stand upon an ugly frog-like head, which represents Mother Earth. Their heads are decorated with huge head-dresses, often with a series of masks representing higher and higher manifestations of the deity. The great *stelae* also have long inscriptions which give all the calendrical information about the time at which they were erected. We are told the exact date, which gods rule the whole day and which command the magic of the night. The phase of the moon is recorded, and sometimes a note about whatever planet was visible is added. These dates are carried forward into the future. If one is to assume that the early Maya followed the same customs as their descendants in the sixteenth century, the inscriptions would have amounted to a statement of the current position and a prophecy of coming events. It was generally assumed at the later date that the fortunes of each of the twenty *Katuns* would repeat in general terms whenever the *Katun* of that number recurred. It amounted to a theory that history would repeat itself in a period of 400 *tuns* (395 years less 274 days). The priests could work out the position of the planets and could count the days to eclipses of the sun or moon, so they could estimate the effect of calendrical change on the total prognostication.

The whole of the art work of the Maya culture from the second century AD until the early tenth century is connected with this wonderfully precise time-measuring system of magic. The power of the priesthood must have been enormous. Even in historic times, when the Spaniards met the Maya, the native rulers belonged to select families whose members as they advanced in age took up alternative priestly and secular functions. They spent life rising from the boy who swept the temple floor, through the young warrior, to the priestly novice, to a war leader, to a high priest, or in special cases to the Halach Uinic, the Ruler of Men. It was an unusual system but of social value since it emphasized the interdependence of power on earth and in the spirit world. There was in later times, at least in Yucatan, a titular overlord who lived in a palatial suite of rooms in the ancient city of Uxmal. They called him the Tutul Xiuh, the Fire Bird (a Mexican title), treated

A page from the Maya Dresden manuscript, thought to date from the 12th century AD. The page represents gods concerned with the movement of fate. In the upper centre a dog carries burning firebrands from the sky. In the middle section the high god Itzamna carries a young goddess in his canoe. The lower register shows different aspects of Itzamna: warrior, water dispenser, prisoner.

him with great respect and even paid a small tribute but took no
notice of his edicts. However, the last one was a sensible man who
made friends with the Spanish conquerors. But in ancient times it
seems that each city was independent, though for a couple of
centuries a group of cities in the Peten district of Guatemala
managed to run with a special kind of calendar in exact
synchronization, as if they were a political unity. Also from the
ancient city of Copan there comes a long sculptured frieze on
which a row of high dignitaries are shown, each wearing a
different breastplate and each seated on a pouffe made up of
hieroglyphs which may represent the names of towns of which
the nobles were the high chiefs or priests.

The whole fantastic culture, with palaces and temples and a few
huge towns such as Tikal, was based on the peasant farmer. No
doubt the calendar complex began as a means of calculating the
right time for planting crops. But the peasant was interested in
planting his maize and beans in the proper way and with a little
ritual to encourage the spirits. He worked hard doing some
hunting while his wife looked after the fields and made pots and
wove textiles. The family made their way to the holy places once
in every twenty days. They prayed and brought offerings for
sacrifice. At least once a year they brought a percentage of their
produce for the service of the temples and as tribute to the chief.
Then they danced and sang in the courtyards at the great
festivals. They did not enter the sacred temples, nor did they
ascend to the god-houses on top of the pyramids. But if it were not
for them, the whole wonderful complex of religion and administration would collapse. It is inconceivable that the artists and
builders would have been free to work their own fields. They
were the servants of the gods and their priests, who would have to
be kept in food and clothing. On the whole it seems probable that
the ancient civilization of the Maya was based on a subservient
peasantry who paid heavy taxes to keep their cities going.

There can be no doubt that the artists who ministered to the
cities were highly skilled and able to interpret the chants of the
priests into pictorial terms. We find through time a gradual
improvement in the quality of the art and only in the early tenth
century, towards the sudden end of the great cities, is there any
trace of decadence. The developed baroque of the eighth and
ninth centuries becomes more florid and less fluent in design. But
it still has a sense of beauty about it. The maize plant flourishes,
and the iridescent green plumes of the Quetzal bird adorn the
heads of the nobles. Written symbols adorn the walls with
beautifully balanced areas of script, and everything seems to have
been going well, when suddenly, one after another, cities cease to

The central plaza in the
Maya city of Palenque, 7th
or 8th century AD. The
observatory tower in the
centre is seen to be
overshadowed by
surrounding buildings.

have inscriptions. The buildings were never destroyed. Sometimes a few have been split open by later earthquakes. A few also have had later walls built inside them over thin layers of vegetable debris. This shows that later groups of Indians had come there to worship the ancient gods. Their crude *incensarios* and the smoke of *pom* incense give proof of their devotion. This is most evident in the ruins of the beautiful city of Palenque.

Maya culture did not end with the abandonment of the sacred buildings. The farmers went on as before. For a few centuries they were under control of the Toltecs in the Yucatan peninsula. Later they were subjugated by the Spaniards, but the people continued with their agricultural life, living in villages and enjoying the

Maya pottery incense
burner with a mask of the
Sun God, from Palenque,
c. 700 AD.

fruits of the earth. The old writing was abandoned only in Spanish times. The old chiefly families continued to receive respect, though on a smaller scale. The aspect of magic in their lives continued too, and still in a few villages there remain elders who cast the fortunes of the coming year by distributing maize grains over the days of a ritual symbolism, much as did their ancestors two millennia ago. The high culture which was abandoned in the tenth century appears to have been the culture of a master caste among the Maya. It is possible that it fell to a popular revolt, but it may have ended because of a belief in the magic of time which dictated mass movements of population, as occurred to the Itza in the early seventeenth century.

Whatever caused the abandonment of the older cities, we must admit that the first phase of Maya civilization was one of the great periods in world art. It is all the more remarkable that it was built in the context of a completely neolithic stone-using culture. There is no trace of the use of metal in this civilization. Even gold was hardly used. In fact, all that remains of gold in the early period is a single bell in the British Museum, and although it was excavated in the ruins of Palenque, it is thought to have been imported from the south. However, though their tools were simple ones of stone and bone, the real strength of Maya culture lay in the skill of the workpeople. They worked to a precise routine, and it appears that the craftsmen were highly specialized. While the mass of the people toiled on their *milpas*, growing maize and beans and keeping flocks of turkeys, the skilled craftsmen lodged near the temples and worked at the creation of beauty for their religion.

The religion was a matter of the passage of time under the care of a series of gods. Each day was under the protection of a god who ruled from sunset to sunrise, and another god who ruled also from sunset, but through to the next sunset. By studying the position of these gods, the priests could define the fortunes of any coming day. They modified their prognostications by allowing for the influence of combinations of deities who ruled the twenty-day periods and the sequence of 360-day *tuns*. Then one added details of the position of the Moon, Venus and some of the other planets. It was all very precise, but of course a good priest could sense the shade of meaning most suited to his client's situation and tone his prophecy to suit. Yet all the Maya believed in the exact mathematical quality of the passage of fate.

Everywhere there is writing, the calendrical system is made clear. But, alas, half the longer inscriptions remain undeciphered. We can read the symbols of time and its passage. Even the conventions of counting in twenties and starting a count with zero, are clear. But there remain many other glyphs which are

undeciphered. There have been many attempts to read them, and progress has been helped by computer studies, but there remains a mysterious area in some of the longer inscriptions which may give us a historical note or two. However, the magics of time passing seem to have satisfied the Maya mind, and they did not really worry about what we should call history. After all, to them it was a matter of progressive fate. From our point of view, although great progress has been made, it still remains a question of which of the eight versions of the Maya language was used, or was it still another variant accepted for religious regions as the sacred language? One is inclined to accept Sir Eric Thompson's view that it was probably close to Chol Maya, but so far it is

Two sections of the 7th-century AD Bonampak frieze, as they have been reconstructed recently.

unproven and so far no attempt to translate the texts in full has been entirely satisfactory.

We do not know the ancient Maya names for their towns. There is probably a clue in that long, high relief frieze from a stairway at Copan on which are depicted a row of nobles seated on pouffes which are also hieroglyphs. These are probably place names. But even if one could decipher the names, it remains to place them geographically so that name and place come together on a map. But there is no reason to suspect that the older Maya had a unified central government. It is probable that there were rather loose federations and that notables were in touch across political boundaries. There must have been much to discuss over the local horoscopes, and attempts to bring about at least an intellectual unification.

For long it was believed, as with so many newly discovered human civilizations, that the Maya were not a warlike people. However, as usual we find that mankind was much more cruel than nature. The importance of armed warrior figures on monuments, and scenes of warfare and conquest, show that the brave and intelligent Maya were a warlike people rejoicing in the taking of prisoners and in the ceremonial slaughter so characteristic of Middle America. The remarkable paintings in the little temple at Bonampak show some account of domestic life and also scenes of battle and the torture of captives. The warriors wear a fantastic variety of costumes, many dressed as god-like figures in masks and plumes. They crowd together in battle, mostly wielding spears which are headed with sharp points of flint, though some are slender lances of pointed palm wood. The decorations of feathers and jade and the dancing postures indicate that war was a matter of glorious enterprise and that warriors were probably mostly men of high social position.

The decorated shoulder-capes, the loincloths and short kilts show the importance which men attached to costume. In another scene we find a princess presenting her child to the chiefs. She and her female companions wear simple, tight-fitting shifts all in fine white cotton. They are held off the shoulders by a draw-string. The skirts of the dresses come to ankle length. Women and the child have their hair pulled back to show the beauty of their carefully moulded skulls. But the main thing to notice about the female costume is its simplicity and delicacy. The fitted gown fastened by an off-shoulder draw-string is to be found in some of the remarkable pottery figurines from the island of Jaina, off the coast of Yucatan. Here the local people seem to have acquired a great skill in modelling and have left us many figurines illustrating the Maya people in all manner of ceremonial costumes. Many of the figurines were limewashed and painted, but in most cases this fragile surface has disappeared and we have just the carefully prepared grey clay surface. In some cases the ladies wear long skirts and shoulder-capes of apparently much heavier material, but the delicate shift garment was also popular. Always the ladies wore necklaces of jade beads, and some wore earplugs, probably of jade, but they were not so splendid as among the noblemen.

Every Maya of importance had a modelled skull. The child resting in his cradle had a light flap of wood resting on his forehead. This slight pressure gradually flattened the frontal bone as it developed. The result was considered by the Maya truly beautiful, for the sloping forehead continued the line of the nose.

Wall painting showing three Mayan dignitaries, from the temple of Bonampak, 7th century AD. The whole of this small temple has been painted with representations of ceremonial life and of war. The thickness of the waistbelts worn by the figures appears to be an indication of their importance.

When the child grew up, the little notch at the top of the nose was filled with a carefully polished piece of jade to perfect the continuity of line. In many cases the back of the skull was bound so that it developed into an egg shape with the point at the back. The hair was also bound back over it and appeared like a sprout of vegetation. Some surviving skulls are so fantastically deformed that one wonders how the Maya nobles functioned; but the evidence is that they were a keen minded and intelligent people. Their priests had skulls fully as deformed as the chiefs, and they were responsible for the remarkable achievement of the Maya calendar. There can be little doubt that these men also planned the layout of the great ceremonial centres, the constant rebuilding of temples and the erection of time-marker monuments.

The usual procedure in making a sacred site was to clear a hilltop and prepare flat areas which were made into courtyards. Usually at one end of the courtyard a pyramid was built, flanked by smaller ones, and on the two sides other pyramids of lesser height were built. The fourth side was often the site of a platform on which a range of smaller rooms was erected. Each pyramid was faced with a steep stairway leading to a temple building, which was made with massive walls far thicker than was actually necessary, supporting a corbelled vaulting. Over this a stone roof, or a steep thatched roof, was built. The stone ones were surmounted by ornamental roof combs, which doubled the height of the structure. The whole building was held together by a strong cement of limestone burned and mixed with a calcareous earth. This set like concrete. As time progressed, more and more concrete was used, and walls were faced with a thick and durable stucco. Up in the Guatemalan highlands the use of sculpture on ceremonial buildings was kept to a minimum, perhaps because their proportions were of importance. They are certainly beautiful in an austere way. But it is also probable that the walls were painted with frescoes in many colours, of which there are no survivors. In the Peten district of Guatemala and in southern Mexico and parts of Honduras, and in British Honduras, the sacred buildings were covered inside and out with finely executed sculptures. In some towns the work was made of stucco which was finished with a lime wash and painted. On the whole it seems that all Maya sculpture was once painted, though little of this work has survived the tropical rains.

As time went on, styles in sculpture changed and gradually assumed a baroque richness. Figures became less static and more realist. Temples were covered by new skins of masonry which enlarged and glorified them. New courtyards were added to the older ones. Ever greater and finer stones marking the passage of

The Pyramid of Kukulcan, crowned by the temple dedicated to Quetzalcoatl, Mayan, 10th to 12th century AD.

time were erected. Some were great vertical *stelae*, a few reaching a little more than twenty feet in height. Others took the form of the great earth monster, a huge lumpy creature modelled on the whistling toad, *rhinophryne dorsalis*. Sometimes altars were placed in front of the time markers, for they represented gods, the Bacabs who supported the four directions of the sky. The east was the direction of Kukulcan, equivalent to the Mexican god Quetzalcoatl, the Morning Star. The south was dedicated to a goddess, probably Ixchel, as a region of the high sun and fertility. The west was the holy place of the ripened corn and of the sunset and was represented by a god equivalent to the Mexican Xipe Totec, who sometimes wears a flayed skin. The north was the black and white region of darkness and bones. Its god was either Ah Puch, lord of death, or an ape-faced god of the North Star. But in some sites the *stelae* all represent one deity, no doubt the magical patron of the place. An example is Palenque where all the gigantic *stelae* wear the great feather capes associated with Kukulcan.

These are but a few of the deities of the Maya pantheon. At the top was Itzamna, the creator, who ruled from beyond the material universe. Below him were gods arranged in degrees of association with the levels of the earth, the sky, the surface of the earth, the material earth itself and the underworld. They march with the twenty days of the calendar. Each flourishes and bears the burden of his time-fate until, at the end of his day, he sits to rest until the recurring of his time. So in turn they all make their parade. The planetary deities, especially the Moon and the planet Venus dance among the days, reflecting their special aspects at the appropriate times.

The Maya astronomers seem to have been excellent observers. They watched their gods moving among the stars, and in the constellations saw shapes which were the houses of their gods.

The observatories were really sighting lines. In a few cases standing *stelae* made lines of sight over a considerable distance, but such observation points seem to have marked the points of sunrise or sunset, though they could be used for noting when a given planet or star group appeared above the sighting point. However, in some enclosed buildings, such as the late Maya Caracol at Chich'en Itzá, windows were arranged so that observations of important points could be made from points where the window opening was the merest slit. There must have been a specialist group of astronomer priests to make the observations. But their work was not coldly scientific. They were primarily concerned with the dance of the gods and read the stories which their masters were enacting in the heavens as a guide to the conduct of mankind on earth.

Maya carved stone head of a god used as an architectural ornament, from Copan, 8th century AD.

No doubt there was a considerable number of technicians attached to the temples. We have no specimens of books of the period of the great cities. They were probably works of great beauty, but none survive. If we are to take the paintings at Bonampak as a clue, they were near realistic representations of gods and ceremonies with painted areas of text. Pottery was of considerable beauty. A whole class of decorated wares seems to have been used for religious purposes, possibly for burials only, since they are nearly all from graves. A whole series of flanged dishes, semi-globular bowls, and high cylindrical beakers were made. The clay was a coarse buff ware tempered with fine sand. No potter's wheel was used, but all the vessels were coiled. This

Painted pottery vessel with image of Camazotz, the Bat God, breathing flames, 9th or 10th century AD.

was made easier by building the clay form on a base made from a broken bowl so that the potter could turn the vessel round as she needed (potters were usually women). However, many of the vessels were painted or moulded with religious scenes. Figures and glyphic symbols were painted in delicate brush strokes in black outline, filled in with tones of red, orange and yellow, rarely with white. The styles change with time, though the basic patterns remain constant. The paintings were made on a base of fine clay slip which had already been burnished and fired. However, there was also a lot of secular pottery which seems always to have been well made and of good shape, though the surface was simply stamped with a ring of patterns or painted with a plain red stripe. A lot of these vessels were totally undecorated, though their simple form was always its own beauty.

Maya woodwork of the older times was very beautifully executed. Little survives, but a great panel of carved zapote wood exists in the Museum at Basel in Switzerland and some fragments from it are in the British Museum. The work, cut with stone chisels and polished with fine sand, is of great beauty as well as technical ability. This panel came from Tikal in Guatemala and is a fine example of the skill of the carvers.

Apparently featherworkers and jewellers formed separate classes. We have no examples of featherwork from the older Maya culture, but from the carvings it seems to have been exquisitely beautiful. The jewellers had no metals but were experts in working hard stones. Apparently the Maya nobles regarded carved jades as important heirlooms. Often we find jades carved in an ancient style in a later grave, and also stones from the highlands are found in the lowland centres and *vice versa*. They made long tubular bugle beads, round ones and some shaped like water melons. But the great works were plaques of fine jade, often worn as pendants. They were carved with religious symbols, which were made by polishing away the surface and cutting grooves by the use of canes dipped in water and then in quartz sand. Thus the hard jade could be slowly polished away. The great skill of the lapidaries achieved a delightful formalized realism in design. Occasionally large plaques of jade were carved, but the rarity of the material and the amount of work required kept down the numbers of these exquisite works of art.

The distribution of ornaments and the nature of the religious buildings makes one conclude that this earlier and very great achievement of culture reflects a strongly aristocratic warrior society. In some ways one could find it paralleled in the social structure of Europe during the Dark Ages, only the Maya had no

Small pottery figure of Maya lady weaving on a backstrap loom, probably 9th century AD. A bird sits on the post to which the loom is tethered.

Pottery figurine showing a Maya warrior with circular shield and neck roll, 9th century AD.

metal. But there was the same emphasis on the war leader and the religious dignitaries. However, the fruits of an ordered society were the time allowed for the development of specialist craftsmen and artists, and the organization of the regular payment of tribute from the mass of the peasant farmers. For some ten centuries this great culture of the Maya advanced in quality, though not in the techniques of ordinary life.

The collapse of this civilization was not instantaneous. We find that there are late carved *stelae* erected in the cities which vary in date over some forty or fifty years. One by one the towns are deserted and overwhelmed by the forest. There is direct evidence for neither war nor pestilence. Do we have to attribute the rapid change in culture to a social upheaval or to some magical ban imposed by the religion? The Maya collapse is earlier than the civil wars of the Toltecs, though indeed Toltec influence was destined to influence the fortunes of the Yucatec Maya to no small degree. It seems that the movements of the Maya are just now beyond our reach. The social revolution in such an early cultural stage seems somewhat unlikely, though indeed the Maya peasants were a stubborn people and very self-sufficient. The magical theory is based on the movements of the Itzá people, but again this is vague and documented only by their mass migration from their last town of Peten Itza.

The lowland Maya of the Yucatan peninsula had a similar collapse of culture, though apparently late in the series. Their largest towns, Uxmal and Chich'en Itzá, belong to the period before the tenth century AD. But it appears that they were never totally abandoned. The Itza, a group whose name translates more easily into Nahuatl where it would mean 'the people of the stone knife', seem to have migrated from the Champoton region in the fifth century and later settled in Chich'en Itzá. But here they were apparently contacted by the refugee Toltec ruler from Tollan. A new Toltec city soon grew on a site to the east of the more ancient Maya town. It was a truly Toltec establishment, and its buildings were all in a truly Toltec style. It is most likely that the Toltecs were a ruling class who were able to command the labour of the indigenous Maya people.

The sculptures at Chich'en Itzá new town are all in a Toltec style but given a rather more realistic tone especially in the *bas reliefs*. There is evidence that the limestone reliefs were all painted in vivid colour. In the British Museum (Ethnography) now the Museum of Mankind, there is a plaster cast which has been painted with a fully documented reconstruction of the original colours. It acquires a totally new impact and shows that the formality of the sculpture in its bare state was once vividly enriched and given life with the work of the artists in colour. The painted wall represented scenes of worship directed towards the great feathered and fire-breathing serpent which was the symbol of Quetzalcoatl among the Toltecs. Importantly it shows that there was a mixture of peoples in Chich'en Itzá, for there are Maya warriors as well as the nobles of the Itza. The painted chamber from which this relief is taken was in the temple associated with the great ball court. Here the Toltec nobles tested the swaying of fate in the game in which the players butted a solid rubber ball with their hips, never using hands or head. The court was divided into four sections representing the four directions of the universe. The teams of highly trained players started with the ball in one court. The team there bounced the ball from one to another, trying to keep it always in their quarter of the court but every now and then endeavouring to butt the ball through a ring set in the wall of the court, some twenty feet above the playing area. If the ball bounced into the quarters occupied by the other team, then they in turn tried to keep the ball bouncing between them. In practice the teams captured the ball from one another quite often, and each in turn tried to score a hit through the ring. The first team to score won the game, and we are told that the spectators ran away, for the winning team had the right to strip them of all their jewels and clothes if they were caught. This was in addition to the wagers of jewellery and splendid clothes which the lords had gambled on their teams.

On the sloping base of the walls of the court at Chich'en Itzá there are representations of a great ball game described in the legends of the Popol Vuh, a Maya story of the adventures of a hero who was the Planet Venus in the underworld. Eventually the hero is captured and his head is cut off by the underworld lords. He is shown with the seven serpents of blood streaming from his neck. The skull was hung up as a trophy, but later, when the beautiful daughter of the Lord of Death was passing by, the skull spat at her heart. She conceived and bore a child who became the Morning Star again. The legend describes the appearance and disappearance of the sacred planet from the sky. It is an amusing modern development that a guide invented an explanation of the carvings, and now visiting tourists are told that the loser (or the winner in some versions of the tale) of the game was decapitated!

But Chich'en Itzá has its own rather gruesome story in fact. A ceremonial stone trackway, poor by comparison with the roads between the more sacred Maya towns, led some nine hundred yards to a great *cenote*, a huge hole in the limestone which has vertical sides some sixty feet deep to the water level of the underground streams in the limestone. The great dark hole was sacred to the rain god, Chac, of the Maya. A temple was built on its edge. There were some owls carved on it, so it was called by its discoverers the Temple of the Owls. It had been painted, and a stone from inside it had been picked up and placed on a wall. Luckily it has been photographed and coloured drawings have been made of it, for tourists are accused of throwing bottles at it for sport, which destroyed the painting. But from the records it has become clear that the picture of a curious little Kululcan in a square sun rising from the horizon, was dated. It was a record of a datable transit of Venus. The date 15 December 1145 gave a check with the recorded Maya date. Thus the despised stone gave us a check which proves the accuracy of the Martinez version of the agreed correlation between the Maya and Christian calendars. But it did nothing to save the lives of human victims thrown into the sacred underworld lake.

There was a story that pretty girls, all maidens, were thrown into the lake. But diving and dredging operations have revealed dozens of skeletons, mostly of elderly or crippled individuals.

One remembers that the Aztecs sacrificed hunchbacks on the occasions of solar eclipses. It seems that there was a story that the victims lived in the world of the rain spirits and that if one was sent back, he would bring a prophecy of the future from the gods. At the time of the sacrifices showers of gold and jade and objects in rubber sacred to the thunder clouds were cast into the water. This had gone on for some centuries when a local chief volunteered for sacrifice. His name was Hunnac Ceel. He disappeared under the dark waters, and four days later he swam to the surface. It was a trick: apparently he had taken a hollow reed through which he could breathe under the water. Perhaps he hid under a limestone ledge. Anyhow, on his reappearance he was almost worshipped and usurped the command of the city. This event in the mid-thirteenth century led to a great disaffection and a rising of the Maya. Eventually the centre of power was changed, and the Toltec establishment moved to the city of Mayapan.

Mayapan is a most unusual phenomenon in ancient America, since it is a walled town. There the local chiefs lived in a state of subjection to Toltec overlords. There are numbers of small temples set in the courtyards of palaces, but the whole place was ill-constructed and appears to be a last relic of the Toltec hegemony. The Maya revolted and wrecked the place. After this the last century of Yucatec Maya history was one of city states each against all the others. They fought, traded, kept calendars and indeed established a truly Maya revival, though their separatism was a hindrance to any great advance. However, ancient tradition was regarded to the extent that titular honours were given to the Tutul Xiuh who lived as an imaginary overlord in a refurbished palace at Uxmal.

It was a rich country which the Spanish visitors discovered at the turn of the fifteenth to sixteenth century. Christopher Columbus met a huge canoe on the high seas south-east of the area now British Honduras. It had a crew of some forty individuals, well dressed and wearing jewellery. The cargo was largely bales of fine cloth. They persuaded the visitors to go towards a rich country to the south. Columbus did so and found only small villages and little of interest. He never met the Maya again. Then in 1512 or perhaps a little later Solis and Pinzón, who had been companions of Columbus, visited the Maya country. They told their story to the historiographer Peter Martyr of Angleria but falsified their sailing directions probably because they had discovered lands of untold riches. But their story is corrected by a map in the book, printed before Cortes discovered Mexico. It shows that the two navigators had sailed round the whole coast of the Maya and Mexican regions and had passed along the Gulf

Late Maya pottery vessel decorated with a god carrying a knife of sacrifice and several rows of human skulls, 9th century AD or later.

coast to Florida. The text of the story given by Peter Martyr mentions the names of several Maya coastal cities and describes the magnificent costumes of the chiefs and the bravery of the spear-wielding Maya warriors in their quilted war-coats. Apparently the traders were very successful.

In 1516–17 the Spanish governor of Cuba, Diego Velasquez, followed up rumours of a rich land to the west and sent an expedition, which returned with a good haul of golden bells and jade. But most important it reported on stone-built cities and a busy people engaged in much inter-tribal trade. There were rumours of a land further north ruled by a great chief. It was called Culhua Mexico. This led, of course, to Cortes's expedition to Mexico. He left Cuba and sailed to the tip of the Yucatan peninsula. A little to the south he landed on the island of Cozumel. There they found small towns and a people having some golden ornaments but living mainly by farming and fishing. They then moved along the northern coast of the peninsula, and visited the Island of Women, so named because they found a small temple there, of which the columns were grotesque figures of kneeling women. There they found fresh flesh from a human sacrifice. They were horrified, even though they had heard of the custom, and hurried away. Then they visited the cities along the coasts of Yucatan and Quintana Roo one after another. They tell us of the fine quality of the buildings, the elaborate clothes of the people, of featherwork and embroideries and of a good deal of gold, of which much was of poor quality. However, they bypassed the Maya, taking with them only a young Spaniard who had been a captive among the Maya and a present of twenty pretty girls given them by a chief. One of those girls was Doña Marina of Mexican fame.

The Spanish conquest of the Maya was never totally complete. But it was in some ways fortunate that the Maya had already divided themselves into separate groups. They had learned the arts of guerilla war in internecine struggles. In Guatemala the Quiché Maya were overthrown by the cruel Pedro de Alvarado and reduced to a sad peonage, though they were always ready to start minor troubles when the chance occurred. In Yucatan Francisco de Montejo commenced the conquest of the separated cities, and his work was continued by his son of the same name. The conquest was often a matter of ceremonial surrender, for the Montejos understood the Maya system and dealt with the titular head of the people, the Tutul Xiuh. Far to the south, by Lake Tayasal, the Itza, living in a world surrounded by deep forest, remained independent until their last mysterious migration in 1697.

Corner of Maya temple at Xlapal, Yucatan, showing masks of the Rain God with projecting snout, 10th or 11th century AD.

There is some Maya history preserved for us in the strange collection of documents known as the *Books of the Jaguar Priest* (*Chilan Balam*). Their texts are written in the Spanish alphabet, though the language is Maya. One of the books was longer than the others and much was hoped from it, but the late Mr Dalgety, an independent researcher, was able to show that it contained four repetitions of the same material. So we are left with a collection of documents which contain a poetic, abbreviated history divided by *Katuns* of a little less than twenty years. They take the forms of prophecy extrapolated from past events. Alas, they all begin with the Toltec period, so we must conclude that the keeping of even a skeletal history was a Mexican introduction and not a truly Maya characteristic.

Mr Dalgety made a long research as a private individual, a true amateur of the subject, into Maya writing, but he died suddenly just before his book was ready for publication. His papers had to be packed up and sent to his brother in New Zealand, so once again the decipherment of the text of Maya writing suffered a setback.

All the surviving Maya books seem to belong to post eleventh-century times. Two have been excavated from older graves, but they are not yet available for study. One is so heavily indurated with lime washed in by rain that it is in effect a solid block of stone. The other works are firstly the *Dresden Codex*, preserved in Dresden, which dates from the twelfth century. It is an elegantly written and beautiful work dealing with divinatory almanacs and having many drawings of the gods of the Maya. A much larger work is the *Codex Tro-Cortesianus*, which is in two separated sections, now in Madrid. It is late in date, probably fourteenth or fifteenth century AD. The subjects are a number of prognosticatory pages, dealing mainly with hunting and bee-keeping, though there are some of a deeper import about creation and the gods. The last of the surviving codices is in Paris; it is the *Codex Peresianus*. Unfortunately this work is much damaged and cannot be handled because of its poor condition. It is a work of theology and places the gods in groups of great significance to the Maya astrologer-priest. As no page is quite complete, it is impossible to draw final conclusions from the text. However, it was obviously once a work of theological importance. It is probably of the fourteenth century. These three documents are at present our only examples of Maya books. They are all of a folded leporello format with pages about eight inches in height and four broad. All are painted on compressed fibrous bark paper.

The technology of the later Maya was by no means as good as that of their ancestors. Their painting was simple, almost crude, their weaving was rather good, but clothing was less elaborate. Even the ladies went topless, though the elderly wore rather pretty ponchos. The men wore the standard equipment of loincloth and sandals, and war chiefs were more elaborately costumed, though much more in Mexican style than the older Maya traditions would lead one to expect. Pottery was simple, much less was modelled, but that cruder work was amazingly alive and graceful in style, though the material was simple grey clay and the modelling was rough. The domestic pottery had become coarser but was still superbly made and of sound practical shapes. In daily life the Maya had lost nothing. It was at the upper end of the social scale that there had been a collapse.

The great advance on early Maya technology was the use of metals. Probably the techniques had a southern origin, but the introduction really came from the Toltecs. A few paintings show what we understand as copper bells worn as fringes of garments. But our real knowledge of Maya metallurgy comes from the treasures dug out of the mud of the sacred well at Chich'en Itzá. Here were bells in copper and also in gold, beads of necklaces and, most remarkable of all, a series of thin sheets of gold which had perhaps been mounted on wood, but when found they were crumpled up. Careful conservation has opened the discs and revealed that they were decorated in *repoussé* with scenes of warriors and sacrifice. They are magnificent works of art and show warriors in both Maya and Toltec costumes. At that period, in the thirteenth and early fourteenth centuries AD, the feathered serpent, identified usually with Quetzalcoatl, takes an important and fearsome position in the designs. In fact the Toltec version of the feathered serpent as displayed among the Maya bears but little resemblance to the later exposition of Quetzalcoatl as the mild Morning Star and the sexy innocence of the Lord of the Winds. However, work in copper and gold was in full swing when the Spaniards invaded Yucatan in the 1540s. Mostly represented by hundreds of little golden cascabels of varying degrees of purity, the workmanship testifies to the continuance of considerable skill in casting, especially in the copper which was a substance very difficult to cast. The carefully burnished surfaces were often enriched with a coating of almost pure gold. Similarly, the golden beads of necklaces were often of a copper-gold alloy enriched by etching out the copper from the surface layer. Many of them were made into heavy necklaces in which the clay core of the beads was retained. Of course they hung very beautifully when worn.

The mass of the people lived in small houses of wood or cane and thatch. They were built on low mounds and were airy, dry and comfortable in the tropical climate. The women kept them spotlessly clean. They also cooked the food, ground maize into flour and made many highly flavoured dishes with chile peppers. Foodstuffs included avocado pears, many kinds of gourd and tropical fruits including the cocoa bean. Meat came from herds of wild peccaries and great flocks of turkeys. All the coastal people were fishermen, using both nets and hooked lines. Women looked after the small fields around the towns and villages, in which they grew not only food stuffs but also cotton and *henequen*. The *henequen* was used for fibres made into ropes and also a coarse cloth, which was made into garments by the poorer people. Many a Maya used waterproof clothing made by covering sheets of *henequen* with melted rubber. The Spaniards learned early how to use this material, but it was another two centuries before the old Maya invention was used in Europe.

The noble families among these later Maya were of great importance and controlled the social life of their cities and the surrounding farms. They exacted a moderate tribute and acted as co-ordinators of the events in the town. In most cases the priests were members of their families, and they also acted as co-ordinators of the calendar which dictated the rhythms of the agricultural year. With this regime life went on very well. The Maya systems of cultivation and farming took up about half the time available, and people lived and loved in a very friendly society. They were totally under subjection to their gods, but the gods were seen as guides and protectors, even those whom we might think of as evil. Sexual morality seems to have been strict, and marriage was regulated by family ties so that matings in too close a degree were not allowed. The national vice was drunkenness, and this was easily accomplished since the local rather runny honey was easily mixed with spices and given a ferment by being washed around the mouths of pretty girls. After a few days the great bowls of *balche*, as it was called, fermented and bubbled for a while before the drink was fit for consumption. At the religious festivals great quantities of fermented liquor were consumed, and people were often seen rolling on the roads or fast asleep and quite hopelessly drunk. It led to a little sexual misconduct, which was rarely regarded as a very serious crime. But the great religious fascination of heavy drinking was that it helped people to be happy during the ceremonies. It was very important that the gods should see that their worshippers were happy because of the gifts they had received. Then they would joyfully send more blessings to their human children.

Once the country had been taken over, the Spanish found that it was an agricultural land and that the Maya gold was all imported from the highlands. The harsh exaction of tribute soon exhausted supplies, and the Maya were left very much as a peasant community of their own devising. They worked for landlords, but they cultivated their own patches of land for their own benefit. Their later history is on a typically Latin American pattern, and for a while it had a series of violent events. One of these was the War of the Castes, but this uprising was suppressed with brutality and was followed by oppressions from foreign land-owners and the profit-grabbers of Porfirio Diaz's regime. It can be said that the Maya returned to comparative freedom only when Mexico became a popular democratic republic. Nowadays the Maya farmer is paid a fair price for his crops, is given modern training in the state agricultural schools and is in a fair way to becoming emancipated from the shadows of past subjection. One wishes that might happen to many other Maya and American Indian communities.

5 The Middle Americans

SOUTH OF MEXICO THE COUNTRY BECAME MORE RUGGED, the forests thickened and the lands narrowed to the Isthmus of Panama, and then it opened again into the broad lands of South America which were either covered with thick rain forests or opened out into highland savannahs. In this vast land there was no history, or at least none that we can recover for within more than a century of the Spanish Conquest. No doubt there was in every town a memory record helped out by some kind of tally, but the white invaders were not told of its contents. We are perforce relying on the researches of the archaeologist rather than the historian.

The tale unfolding is exceedingly complex and shockingly incomplete. However, a number of researchers in the last half century have made several areas clear, and the linguists have established the complexity of the problems involved. For one thing, the Indians of the area spoke many different languages. Nowhere is there any continuous linkage between groups speaking similar tongues. The whole area seems to have been the scene of periodic two-way migrations, probably not peaceful ones. The peaks of civilization were reached in plateaux in the north and on isolated stretches of coast in Panama, while in the far south fortified villages along the river valleys and the high plateau were the centres. All the peoples cultivated the ground. All had maize, but many in the south relied much more on starch from the manioc roots. Maize moved southwards from Mexico in quite early times, reaching as far as Peru by 1,000 BC. Manioc moved up from the Caribbean coasts, reaching into San Salvador a few centuries later. Quinoa from Peru also spread into the South American highlands in early times. But nowhere were the conditions such that a tribe could develop a high culture in isolation, and nowhere was there a chieftainship, except among the Colombian Chibcha, strong enough to dominate the neighbouring tribes. But everywhere there were areas of high art where handmade ceramics were beautiful, and gold ornaments plentiful. This region was a golden land of incredible wealth.

Painted vase in the form of a jaguar, from southern Costa Rica, 14th or 15th century AD. The cuts in its arms and legs were to permit gases to escape during firing.

The native peoples regarded gold as something most beautiful and magical. It was used properly as material for ornament. In some areas it marked social worth; in others all apparently could wear gold of great purity. Most of the pendant figures were images of deities in the forms of animals, often of great elaboration. One is astonished at the skill of the jewellers who cast these figures all in one piece, with several little pendant plaques hooked onto them. In the earlier periods the gold was either hammered or cast, but someone, probably in Costa Rica or Panama, discovered the possibilities of mercury as an amalgam. Thus, before the arrival of the Spaniards an immense variety of work was produced.

There was little mining for gold. The greatest quantities were placer-washed from the sands of river beds. But in a few places it seems that exposed veins of gold-bearing rocks were dug out in an open-cast area, crushed and washed. But this was not common and never used where very hard stone was involved. Smelting was on a very small scale through the whole area, just a crucible holding a couple of pounds of gold at the most. Fires were of wood and charcoal. The heat was worked up by the goldsmith's apprentices blowing the fire through copper tubes. Nowhere were the bellows discovered. Various types of wax were used in making the models which were to be cast. In many cases vegetable wax or even rubber was used, since the native beeswax tended to be very soft and almost liquid. In reality the arts of the goldsmiths were very limited from the technological angle, but their skill in preparing their work was remarkable. Nowhere in the Middle American area were scales in use, so when the smiths prepared the copper-gold alloys, they worked by estimation. It is not surprising that no two articles of goldsmiths' work have precisely the same composition.

Except for the Colombian Muisca (Chibcha) there was a considerable uniformity in skills, with perhaps the Quimbaya of the Cauca Valley being the great masters in the goldsmith's art. But uniformity of style does not mean any uniformity of culture. The tribes varied enormously. Many went naked except for paint; others wove cotton into simple skirts and loincloths. We know practically nothing about the nature of government. Probably many tribes had elective chiefs, but others had reached the status of hereditary chieftainship and regulated social classes.

We now know that the whole of Middle America was populated by 2,000 BC and that the main cultural influences from earlier times came from the shores of Venezuela and Colombia. Owing to the roughness of the terrain, it is probable that the early contacts were made by canoemen moving around the coasts. But

Golden pectoral showing two warriors with clubs and spear-throwers, from Panama, 12th or 13th century AD.

there were also cultural movements from the north, since maize had already reached the Peruvian coast by this date of 2,000 BC. This also was probably in large part a coastal movement. The carriers of the farming tradition would have settled here and there. As the soil leached out, they may well have preferred to move to other coastal sites rather than tackle the frightening fertility of the inland forests. Of course, there were earlier human inhabitants, small bands of hunters working on foot to gather enough food to survive. They left no noticeable effect on the later populations.

The working of gold seems on the whole to have moved up from the *cordilleras* of the Andes into the Colombian region and thence into the areas to the north. Although the methods of working were comparatively primitive, the technical ability of the local populations was very considerable. Objects of great beauty have been found, nearly all in burials, showing a wealth in gold undreamed of by early Europeans. However, it is to be remarked that to the American Indians gold was a thing of beauty. Its value as ornament was supreme, and there is evidence that special pieces were traded far from their place of origin. This is

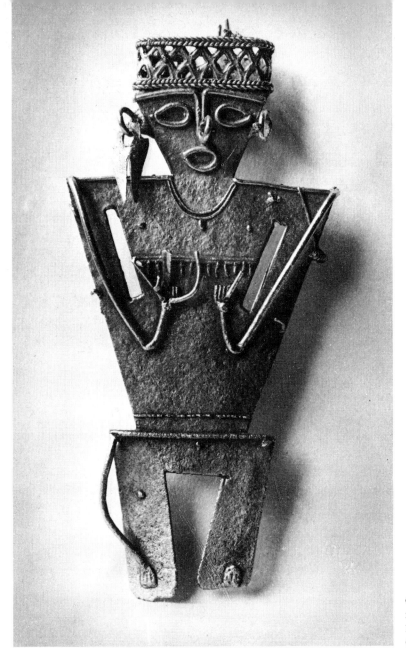

Chibcha golden plaque representing the Sacred Eldorado, from Bogota, Colombia, 15th century AD.

easy to discover, since each area had a distinctive local style. The evidence shows that gold-working began around five hundred years before the beginning of the Christian era and that in the richest areas of Panama and Costa Rica the peak of metal working was reached in the tenth to twelfth centuries AD. Whether this implies a breakdown in civilization in the two centuries before the Spanish conquest is not clear. We must remember that both war and trade were endemic activities in the region.

The whole area is lacking in native history. There seems to have been some kind of record kept, as in modern times the Cuna

Indians of Panama keep traditions in pictorial manuscript form. But of pre-Columbian times we have no records. None of the many tribes had any known set of meaningful glyphs. Traditions among the Chibcha of Colombia go back for some five generations of their chiefs. But even there we are dependent on the word of Spanish adventurers rather than of native documents.

The Spanish began with a misconception. It was thought that there was no land between Spain and China. So they thought that once they had sailed westwards, the riches of the East would be open to them. They dreamed of trade with a China like that visited by Marco Polo two centuries earlier. So they were hoping for gold. Christopher Columbus sailed out to the Indies and found a charming race of naked Indians. Some of them wore ornaments of gold. The stools of chiefs were inlaid with gold. Girls wore necklaces of golden beads and a similar anklet on their right leg. On great occasions the ladies left off their little aprons and wore a single bead of green stone in front of their *mons veneris*. Jade, thought the visitors. But, alas, the gold and some of the men and girls were all the treasures that Columbus brought back in 1492. And the golden beads were made of pottery coated with gold.

On each of his four voyages Columbus sailed a little further south, and though he found more golden trinkets, illness and bad luck followed him. But the discoveries had unleashed Spanish greed. First the West Indies were ransacked and their peoples enslaved. Thousands of the natives committed suicide rather than work for the cruel white man. True, half of them were Caribs and cannibals who had eaten their way into the islands from the South American coasts, but that was not the entire story, since the Arawaks were a more peaceful race and had been in the islands for some fifteen centuries before the Carib invasion which was still going on when Columbus arrived. All of them worked placer mines in river sands for their ornaments. Otherwise they made fine pottery and carved wonderfully, depicting their gods in splendid wood carvings and making strange low stools for their chiefs. Occasionally they used stone chisels for making standing figures, but this was not very common. They were a simple farming and fisher folk. They had not moved much in the ways of civilization over a thousand years, but they were well fed and happy until the blight of the plantations was imposed on them.

The Spaniards next began to find that there was a continent between them and the Far East. They sought for a channel to take them over. In Middle America they found gold in Tierra Firme and Veraguas, gold beyond their dreams possessed by simple Indian tribes of cannibals living in small towns of wooden huts. They robbed and killed many of them. Others they made into slaves.

Then came Balboa. He was fired with the desire to see the fabled
South Seas. So, with a convoy of soldiers and Indian baggage-
carriers, he climbed through the jungles and came out on the
shores of a new sea. He astonished the natives by erecting a cross
in the water and claiming that he had discovered the sea, the one
which they had been navigating in their canoes for untold ages.
Then Balboa returned. Pedrarias Davila was the Governor and,
being jealous, he had Balboa beheaded. That stopped nothing.
The systematic exploration of the Golden Lands was on, and the
gold soon went to be melted down and sent to the Royal Treasury
in Madrid.

That was an end of beginnings. But we must look at the regional
archaeology of days before history. It is best to work our way
southwards from the lands of the Maya.

The influence of Maya styles and traditions was very important
in the adjacent areas of San Salvador and Honduras. The main
thrust was along the highlands, but from the Ulua Valley we find
Maya-style pottery and a series of beautiful white marble vases
which echo Maya shapes but have no trace of glyphs. Throughout
San Salvador there are many traces of an early movement
northwards which probably reflects the advance of the Pipiles.
Then, in the great area of Honduras, we find a weakening Maya
influence as we approach the Atlantic coast. There the Mosquito
Indians made good solid hand-coiled pottery, strong rather than
beautiful. They also carved fine stone bowls, very massive and
straightforward in form, with upright sides, having a band of
geometric ornament at top and bottom and standing on tripod
legs. Many of them had lugs for lifting in the form of animals. The
great expanses of Nicaragua, a region of mountain and forest,
were once controlled by the Nicarao, but little research into their
past has been undertaken in the last century. Some earlier
explorers found great stone figures nearly life size, a few showing
men with alligator heads or with alligators on their backs. Here
and there among groups of mounds which once supported
wooden palaces great stone balls have been found, many standing
on plinths and all without any legend or meaning. They were very
accurately made, but there is no account of their making, no
records of their makers and, as far as one knows, no one has said
that they were made by visitors from outer space.

On the Atlantic coast leading down through Costa Rica, the
Guetar Indians held sway. They were master craftsmen in stone
and made fine figures of jaguars and jaguar men, usually under a
metre in height, always active and lifelike. They lived in a land of
forests where the jaguar and alligator abounded. These creatures
were forces of terror to the Indian farmers of the region, and so

Phallic Guetar stone figure
of a god carrying a war
club, from north-eastern
Costa Rica, 10th or 11th
century AD.

Carved marble vase, from
the Ulua Valley in northern
Nicaragua, between 13th
and 15th centuries AD.

Head of a standing stone figure, from central Costa Rica, 14th or 15th century AD.

their spirit forms had to be placated to help people retain a sense of security.

The stone tables used for grinding maize and other seeds for food become more elaborate, and assume magnificent forms which remind one of the upcurved wooden *duhos* of the West Indies, only these *metates* often end in symbolic crocodile heads. They appear to be earlier and stronger in design than many other stools made in animal form, such as jaguars and monkeys. Sometimes in the highlands of Costa Rica they assume elaborate forms with numbers of intertwined animals forming an openwork substructure to the grinding surface. Here one senses a high civilization with a chiefly caste dedicated to a religion of the dangerous powers of nature and owning these incredible specimens of stone technology. They vary from the strong forms of Nicaraguan work especially from around Lake Omotepec, to the rich complexities from further south around Cartago in Costa Rica. Both groups have been dated between 1000 and 1250 AD. But one must conclude that they are expressions of an idea common to two differing cultures. The stones used in the region are all of volcanic rock, and many are granular in quality, so they can easily be shaped, but also retain a natural roughness.

There is a similarity about most work from Costa Rica and Panama, but local styles are recognizable and local languages are very distinct from one another. It seems that there was a good deal of trading as well as fighting, and that people copied one another's techniques. On the whole, one may say that the coastal regions were the sites of the higher civilizations and that the forested mountain regions were the refuge of less advanced tribes who had been driven to take shelter among the rocks and trees. Clothing was mainly in the form of short skirts and loincloths, but jewellery and feather ornaments were plentiful. Of course, body painting was resorted to in a thoroughly American Indian manner, and we have evidence for the patterns in the form of painted pottery figurines and the designs on sculptured figures.

OVERLEAF Elaborate stone metate with carving representing monkeys, from central Costa Rica, 13th or 14th century AD.

It appears that the main deities of these more civilized southerners were of a primitive type of power-wielders of earth and sky, for we find images of alligator and jaguar deities, of monkey gods and of wide winged birds. These beings may sometimes be carrying human heads, and they may carry serpents in their hands. All these characteristics are of a southern aspect and may well be linked with the deities of the coastal peoples of Peru. The whole aspect is thoroughly of the natural world, and its animality is different in quality from the religious art of Mexicans and Maya. We are still in Central America but the arts have become thoroughly South American in aspect.

One of the great art centres of the region was the Nicoya peninsula on the Pacific coast of Costa Rica. Here a group of villages rather than a large town subsisted on fishing and agriculture of the usual type of slash-and-burn cultivation. The possibility of a settled life seems to have made the area a centre of the arts for nearly two millennia. There are changes in culture, differences in pottery through time and an increasing use of gold up to the thirteenth century, after which culture declined.

An important product of Nicoya was a series of club heads made from hard green stones. These are not just hammer-heads in type but are elaborately carved to represent animal and human heads. They are in great variety, but realism is subjected to a simplification into planes and areas of decoration. The quality of the design and the impression of strength given by the heads make them into very desirable items for modern collectors. There is in consequence a constant danger of unscientific grave robbing, as in many other areas of Middle America. However, as well as the club heads, there are numbers of jade 'axe blades' of great beauty. They are usually in the form of a human head, sometimes with head ornaments, and a torso of which the arms are folded across the waist. From the waist the figure becomes an axe blade of a smoothly curved shape. The end is polished to a high degree of sharpness. It has been suggested that, while the figures could be mounted as axes, they may well have been used as knives in

Stone offering table supported by human figures, from Chiriqui, Panama, 14th or 15th century AD.

which the figure was the hand-grip and the cutting edge was sliced across the wood or leather to be cut.

The development of gold as a form of ornament moves from cut plates up to finely modelled wax castings, often of bells reflecting the jade-axe designs, with a figurine in high relief, often a monkey, from which the bulbous bell descends. The metalwork follows the usual Middle American pattern in which the object is modelled in a plastic substance such as wax or rubber and then replaced by metal in *cire-perdue* casting. Many composite objects were made in which pendants were hung on the main figure by means of thick gold wire hooks.

In central Costa Rica a rich culture existed around Cartago, but our knowledge comes almost entirely from grave finds. There was fine gold work, jade and a magnificent series of pottery vessels in several styles dating from the early centuries of the Christian era. The finest work seems to date from just before 1000 AD, but there are later developments of fine quality in which cream, red and black painted figurines become frequent. They are, however, simpler than the finest of the Nicoya pieces.

We next reach the Republic of Panama, a narrow ridge of tumbled mountains once entirely covered with thick forest. The centres of high culture in ancient times were on the Pacific coast. Traders in dug-out canoes moved easily along that coast, and the local groups of people were also fishermen. The basic plant foods were cassava and maize, but there were also many fruits including the coconut. So life was comparatively easy. The main drawback to developing civilization was inter-tribal war. Also, in the heavy tropical rains, the minerals were rapidly leached out of the soil exposed by cultivation.

The native peoples in the mountains lived in villages, and their huts of cane and leaf thatch were cool and reasonably dry. They had hereditary chiefs who wore ornaments of gold and a gold-copper alloy. Most people went naked, though on great occasions they painted their bodies with rich designs which looked like over-all tapestry. They were the ancestors of the Cuna Indians of today, whose women make appliqué textiles covered with designs which mostly reproduce the ancient painted patterns. They recently made books of long strips of vegetable fibre in which strings of pictures recorded events, but we do not know if such records were painted in ancient times. Now the Cuna mostly live along the Atlantic coasts.

The heights of local civilization were reached by the peoples of the Pacific coasts. The highest expressions of human endeavour come from the Veraguas coast and the peninsula of Chiriqui. This region includes some islands from which the Spaniards found the

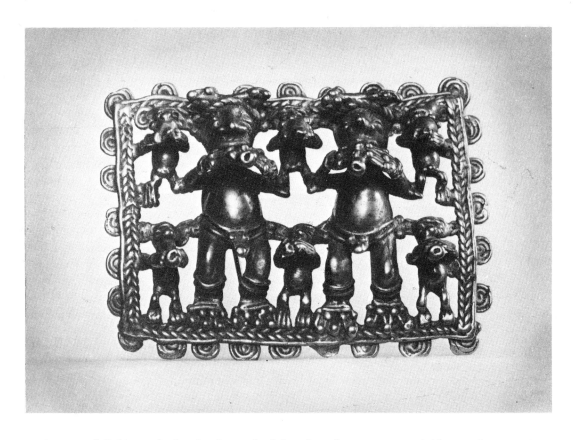

natives pearl-fishing. The local cultures had developed over some two millennia, and as usual they show development at first but then changed little when craftsmen had achieved a good level of handiwork. There were no machines used in any part of the area. All pottery was hand coiled and fired in an open brushwood bonfire. There appears to have been considerable care in piling the pots, since there are comparatively few burn marks. Plentiful supplies of gold were washed out from river sands. The *cire-perdue* castings are unusually rich in artistic quality. Sometimes pendants of some six by four inches were made. They had suspension loops and a guilloche frame. Within them the figures of men, alligators and jaguars seem to dance. The figures are all naked except for a belt, and each figure displays a bare penis, with in many cases the glans uncovered. Feminine figures are less common but they are usually naked. Stone figures also exist from the region, in which the women wear wrap-around skirts.

The most perfect pottery from the area was made in the centuries around 1000 AD on the northern part of the Veraguas coast. Here the vases are of simple parabolic section, even and thin, and perfectly fired. The surface is matt, and the colour a

Gold pectoral representing a group of musicians playing flutes and ocarinas, from Chiriqui, Panama, probably 15th or 16th century AD.

simple khaki tone. Sometimes angular strap-handles are fitted, and one finds applied ornament in the form of tiny animals, often monkeys, in the joints. Some vessels have hollow legs which are slit and contain clay pellets to form a rattle. This has been called armadillo ware, probably because many of the earlier pieces were in the form of armadillos. It is in form and general quality probably the finest pottery ever made in pre-Columbian America.

Further south, in the Chiriqui peninsula, there is much more colour and a fantastic variety of design. Jaguar men dance in gold among the bells; musicians play on flutes and ocarinas on little golden plaques to be worn in ears and nose. Thousands of golden bells come from graves where they were obviously once the tinkling fringes of garments. Pearls were worn as necklets and wristlets. The potters made many little figures of animals all brightly painted in cream, red, black and a grey-blue. Many dishes were painted all over in a welter of design upon design. Dancing figures of the jaguar man and alligator man, or mixtures of these, are drawn on a background of stripes in several colours. The design fits the area of the plate quite wonderfully, and in fact it probably represents the designs which the weavers made for the scanty clothing worn. But the damp tropical climate prevented anything of the weavers' art surviving.

The whole area of Chiriqui was the centre of a village civilization of high quality. The living must have been very good indeed, with fishing and tropical farming. The area has been well investigated by archaeologists, and the deposits divided into several time-layers. The richest period was around 1200 AD, and there was some deterioration later. Changes of style in the past probably indicate the passage of tribes from the north towards the Colombian area, and from Colombia outwards into the north. Chiriqui was fortunate in many ways, and it was apparently an area which was able to stand the passage of other tribes without a great loss of culture. One must remember that the warriors who passed that way were armed with spears, bows and arrows, and stone clubs. They were formidable enough, but defences against them were relatively easy to contruct. Much depended on the efficient organization of watchmen and of informants in the parties of traders who ventured up and down the coasts.

It was in this region that the Spaniards heard first of a marvellous gold land to the south which proved later to be Peru.

From the south of Panama the prospects of the American Indians opened out into the wide continent of South America. The early hunters penetrated the highland zones rather than the swampy coastal regions of the Pacific and spread along the Atlantic coasts, though there are few remains of their passage. The coasts of Venezuela and Colombia have yielded fragments of simple pottery vessels which seem to be the earliest ceramics in the Americas, dating to before 3000 BC. Archaeologists are now working at sites well inland which seem to have been the areas where pot-making originated in the Americas. The art spread and apparently went westwards as well, to influence people on the coasts of Ecuador, who were making simple pots and figurines of women about 2200 BC, long before the Jomon culture of Japan, to which they have been compared, had developed. The existence of ceramics implies a settled community, since ceramics are of no use to a mobile hunting population because of their fragility. This very early South American ceramic tradition is a marker of the early development of agriculture. It is axiomatic that an agricultural community lived in houses, and we might expect much woodwork, but the climate of northern South America is one of heavy rainfall and so woodwork has hardly survived apart from some finely carved houseposts from Ecuador. Stonework, apart from tools and weapons, is rare.

The most remarkable stone sculpture from our area comes from the southern central highlands of Colombia. There a remarkable collection of dolmen-like tombs and temples, having great carvings of men and animals, centres around San Augustín. They are now known to be rather early in date, from about 500 BC to 250 AD. These most expressive works show some figures of tusked warriors carrying shields and wearing animal-form helmets. But some figures have the warrior probably marked as a deity by the tusks in his mouth, with a separate animal-form over

Luna-ware vase from Lake Ometepec, Costa Rica, 12th or 13th century AD.

Standing dish painted with crocodile images from Chiriqui, Panama, 13th century AD.

his head as if it were his inspiring spirit. There are many variations in style among these figures, but each one has a quality of strength and life which marks the San Augustín culture as a great centre of American Indian art.

All areas where there has been proper investigation show a sequence of cultures which have been farming communities for a long period commencing around 3000 BC. Areas expand or contract; changes of style mark the coming and passing of peoples without names for us. Many of the investigations made have been due to haphazard discoveries and the depredations of tomb-robbers. Hence there is no clear archaeological continuity. But it is plain that in this terrain of the mountainous rain forests there has never been a unified imperial culture such as those of Peru and Mexico.

The nearest attempt at forming a dominion appears to be that of the Chibcha of the grassy plateau of highland Colombia, around Bogotá and Tunja. The people kept an outline history, in which

Stone figure of a deity from San Augustín, Colombia, late BC or early AD.

they had verbal record of the exploits of four generations of their high chiefs. They had a belief that they had always lived on their high plateau around the sacred Lake Guatavita. Here the waters of the great flood had driven their ancestors higher and higher. The creators had turned themselves into two golden serpents who dived into the lake. Bochica, their principal culture hero, had appeared and opened the walls of the crater lake so that the waters ran away and the Chibcha were saved. Thenceforward every new high chief was taken to the lake to make an offering of gold to the spirits below. He was rolled in clay and then in gold dust. He jumped into the lake and washed off the deposit so that the gold filtered like a glistening cloud down into the depths. The high chief ruled by the power of the sun and was surrounded by several wives and a court of noblemen.

Every year an expedition was sent into the forests to the east to capture boys from the wild forest Indians for sacrifice to the sun. The boy was cared for, and when his year of captivity came to an end, he was tied to a rock exposed to the sun. He died and his soul took messages to the heavens asking for help for the Chibcha. But sometimes a Chibcha girl would take pity on the boy and, if he could achieve sexual intercourse with her, he was set free and another victim was slain. Everywhere the Chibcha forces went, the leaders wore golden birds as pendants. On the war path a larger eagle of gold was set up on top of a post. Sometimes, of course, high ranking officers were slain by the forest people. It was a golden eagle from such a victim that Sir Walter Raleigh obtained in Guiana. He wore it on his neck while imprisoned in the Tower of London as proof that he had been to the land of Eldorado.

In the arts the Chibcha expressed a preference for matt surfaces. Their pottery vessels include many figures of chiefs and their wives, highly formalized and painted in white and black. Always the highly skilled coiling is left unburnished. Similarly with the golden figurines, mostly flat plaques with features and weapons added as strips of wire. Sometimes these flat figures are mounted vertically on a base plate so that a scene is created telling a story. Often one sees the High Chief carried in a hammock or else with priests and nobles on a raft.

A particularly important aspect of this rough surfaced gold work is its colour. The Chibcha were skilled metallurgists and made many figures of gold in alloy with differing amounts of copper, so that the results vary from pure copper colour up to the beautiful pale yellow gold. It appears that they were worn to indicate the social rank of an individual. The purer the gold, the higher the rank.

Pottery figure of the high chief of the Chibcha, from Bogotá, Columbia, 15th century AD.

The Chibcha also wove fine cloth from native cotton. This is very rare, but a sheet in the British Museum is painted with typical Chibcha designs and a repeated pattern of the seated sun god Bochica. The colours are pale green, brown and cream on white cloth. It is sad that so little of this fine material survives.

Chibcha houses were conical roofed with walls of timber and cane. Sometimes the timber was carved and gilded. The Spaniards mention a great palace for the chief with many divisions. The whole compound was the royal palace, including other similar but smaller huts for the great dignitaries. Such a palace and such houses were quite sufficient to withstand the weather of the highland savannahs.

To the west of the Chibcha-speaking peoples, Colombia was divided by two great river valleys descending from the high mountains to the south-west of the country which were part of the Andes. These are the Cauca and Magdalena, which in the lowlands join to make the Sinu which flows out into the Caribbean at the great port of Barranquilla. These rivers flowing through the wooded mountain ranges of the Andean chain were the homes of several smallish tribes, who between them produced the richest gold work of the Americas. Their chiefs, although none ruled wide areas, seem to have been autocrats who lived in great state. They were decorated with gold; their palaces were of timber but full of golden vessels. The river also produced many grains of grey platinum, of which the local people made practical

Small golden frog, from Colombia, between 12th and 14th centuries AD.

use. They heated the granules and hammered them into fish-hooks. The gold they kept for its regal beauty. One notes that each group of villages had its own style of work, and modern studies have differentiated between them. All of them differ entirely in style from the work of the Chibcha. In fact the Chibcha never seem to have raided towards these western valleys. In any case, the Magdalena was a natural barrier defending the people who lived mostly to the west, in the valley of the Cauca. The lands were forest-covered and probably unhealthy even before the deadly mosquito carrier of diseases was brought in during the sixteenth century.

In the period when Inca Peru was still in its death throes, Spanish adventurers took considerable forces through these valleys to go to golden Peru. They record their experiences of tribes of painted savages, of cane and timber palisaded villages, of primitive savagery and yet of a kind of glory, though in their time the civilizations were in a state of decline, probably through intertribal wars. They tell a horrible tale of the artistic Quimbaya people specially breeding babies so that they could enjoy the delicate flesh in cannibal feasts. But all those tribes were cannibals, and their golden masks show that they filed their teeth, so that a mouth must have looked frighteningly like a row of shark teeth. There is beauty and cruelty in the faces of their work. As well as different styles in their gold, there is no unity in the quality and form of their pottery. The whole of the great river valleys seems to have been always divided among many tribes, all at war with one another and all cannibals. Yet when one contemplates their work, one is astonished at the beauty of form and surface they achieved. The Quimbaya in particular made figure vases from gold. As they were made for the ruling classes, the figures are naked. Among them nakedness was testimony to social importance. Only people who had to labour among the thorns of field and forest wore skirts to protect their delicate genitals. The nobility displayed their beauty openly with necklets, head ornaments and bangles on legs and arms, all of gold on their light brown skins. When the Spaniards met their descendants, they wore war paint, often of black dye, and were less prepossessing.

The cultures of the river valleys of Colombia from north to south include the following: the Tairona, around the mouths of the rivers; the Quimbaya, in the middle reaches; then to the south-west the Calima style and to the south-east the Sinu culture. There appears to have been a great deal of trade between the various areas, and a Sinú object was found among the treasures dredged from the *cenote* at Chich'en Itzá in Yucatan, thus giving a

Seated figure of a Quimbaya lady showing body paint, from the Cauca River Valley, Colombia, 15th century AD.

twelfth-century date for the style. Several Quimbaya objects have been reported from Panama.

The Tairona lived in considerable settlements near the mouth of the river system. Their wooden houses in the villages were surrounded by stone-paved walkways, and the village squares were also paved. A few houses had lower walls of rough masonry. The people had simple golden ornaments, many derived from trade from the south. Their pottery is coarse and tough, but sometimes it echoes ideas from inland. In a few cases figures of animals have been made as a common spout for groups of four small globular vessels. It is in Tairona country that the settlement of Puerto Hormiga was discovered, with pottery antedating 3000 BC, but there is no hint of any continuity from those early times. After the Spanish Conquest, the Tairona took the destruction and loss of independence as a visitation from their gods. They voluntarily abandoned the cultivation of maize in the terraces they had made around their villages.

In the middle Cauca region the Quimbaya cannibals had inhabited the area for some centuries, having a high point in their arts about the eleventh or twelfth century AD. They were masters in the arts of gold-working and potting. Pottery vessels of a buff ware were painted all over with a pale cream slip and then coated with wax cut into patterns; this was dipped in a bath of black dye. The wax was melted off to show a resist dyed pattern in black. In many cases the process was repeated with a red dye, thus producing a pot of three colours. Apparently, like the Peruvians, they dyed textiles with this form of batik work, though only a few threads have survived. Another ceramic form was of pottery bowls made of thick clay which was carved with geometric patterns in imitation of chip-carved wooden vessels. The surface was then burnished, and the pot was fired.

In all probability these skilled potters were the women. They would work in their cane cabins in the villages perched on eminences just above the river. Most of their implements were made of wood, though the men made beautifully polished stone axe-blades and chisels. Apparently the larger huts of chiefs were filled with wooden utensils, ornaments and vessels of gold. The excavations of graves have yielded vast quantities of golden bottles and figures of the most exquisite workmanship. They come from tomb chambers at the foot of vertical shafts and were so well hidden that it has taken all the skills of modern tomb robbers to get at the treasures before the serious archaeologists have been able to investigate them. The forms are graceful; the system of manufacture, even for large bottles and figures sometimes eight or nine inches in height, was *cire-perdue* casting.

Gold pendant ceremonial knife from the upper Cauca Valley, Colombia, (?)12th century AD.

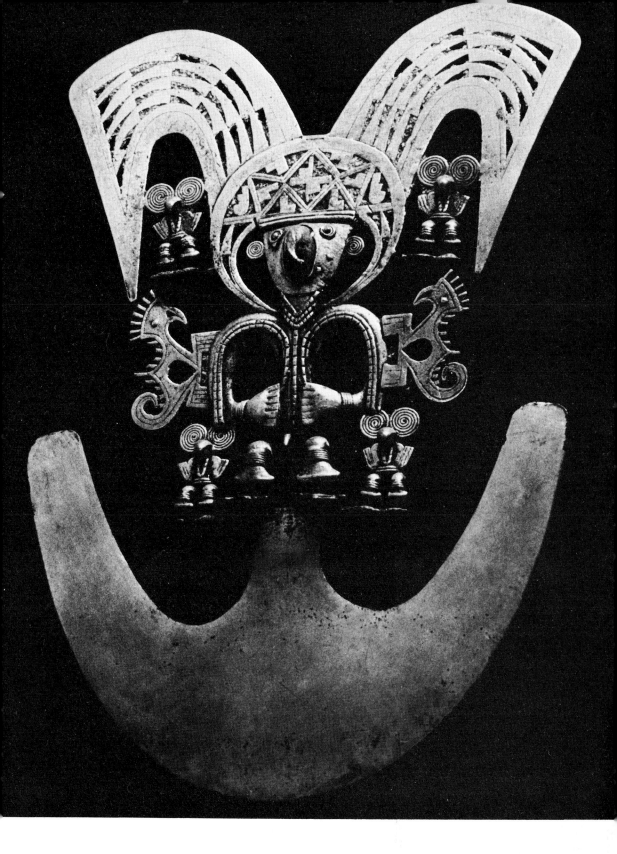

Calima-style repoussé gold plate with male figure, Colombia, between 12th and 14th centuries AD.

Some are of pure gold, which was plentiful in the river sands of the region, but many are of a mixture of gold and copper which has a lower melting-point. After casting was complete, the vessel was washed over with a strong vegetable acid which dissolved away the copper in the surface layer of the object. Then it was burnished and had all the appearance of a solid golden vessel.

The great skills of the metal workers suggest that they were a separate social caste who had leisure to specialize in their technologies. Certainly the Quimbaya were artists of great ability who produced a kind of beauty which the Western mind can easily appreciate. One of the Spanish *conquistadores* said that if the tribes of Colombia had a united government, its riches would far exceed the treasures of the Incas.

From the Calima region, not far away though separated from the Quimbaya territory by tremendous ravines and forested mountains, comes more gold. This was worked up into huge breast-plates some twelve inches wide and nine in depth. The centre of each breastplate was decorated with a human mask in high relief, and the curved edges were marked by a linear pattern, which is a repetition of small unit designs. Some people have suggested that the designs had a calendrical meaning, but this is very doubtful. Most often the masks are reposeful representations of men with curved noses in which the septum has been pierced for wearing a pendant ornament. Such ornaments were worn all over Colombia and varied a great deal in design, from massive outlines to the most delicate filigree work. From this region come curious golden figures of gods with cast openwork head-dresses. They are the handles of ceremonial knives. Some of them show a layered structure as if a layer of gold foil had been pressed on to a copper-gold base while very hot. This process is not unlike the Sheffield-plating. The figure towers up amid several layers of animal figures. The shape of the head-dress suggests that it may be a moon deity, but we have no records of the religion behind the patterns. We can only admire their rhythmic designs and high quality.

From around the town of Darien in northern Colombia come a number of golden objects which have an interesting inde-terminate form. A pair of flat legs and a narrow body are surmounted by a mask-like form made of highly decorative designs almost like strips of wire work. This is surmounted by two domes in the form of human breasts. The meanings are not known, but the figurines are very widely distributed through the gold-using regions far to the north.

In the far south, the complex and decorative pierced plaques of the Sinú culture come from the high mountains bordering on the

centres of the Andean borders with Ecuador. The land is verging
on a drier and more unified region which has, however, little
history. But at least the coastal regions of Ecuador have more data
from excavation. These coasts have less of the terrible rain forest,
with its mangrove swamps and torrential small rivers which make
the Pacific coast of Colombia so uncertain a place for human life. It
appears that in ancient times canoe-men skirted it, perhaps just
camping in a river mouth as they made their way along the coast.
As one reaches the Ecuadorian coast, the country becomes less
permanently wet. The rainfall becomes seasonable and the forest
thinner. Southwards along the coast the climate becomes much
drier and the countryside more and more open, a prelude to the
dry coasts of Peru.

In pre-Colombian times, the Scyri of Quito ruled the southern
part of Ecuador in some state. His power was great; the kingdom,
rather poor in art, was rich in gold, and it tempted the last Inca but
one to conquer it. In fact the ill-fated and villainous Atahuallpa,
last ruler of Peru, was the son of the Inca conqueror Huayna
Ccapac and a princess of Quito. But this is all late in time.

The coasts of Ecuador had been the site of farming cultures
which began producing pottery in the beginning of the third
millennium BC. Already the people were wearing clothing, a
wrap-around skirt, longer for women than for men. The pottery is
crude, scraped up out of a small lump of clay, but it marks a
cultural step forward from about 3200 BC. The area is quite small,
around Valdivia in about the middle of the Ecuadorian coast. The
Valdivia culture is succeeded by the much more widespread
Chorrera culture, dating from 1800 BC to about 500 AD. In this
period new intrusive cultures begin to appear by 800 BC, and by
500 BC there is a cluster of Ecuadorian cultures all on the Pacific
coast. At this point there was the appearance of gold work, at first
in flat sheet but rapidly assuming three dimensional forms. Resist
dyed pottery was also introduced. In the highlands the first large
area culture was the Tuncahuan, which lasted from 800 BC to
about 500 AD.

One of the most curious and artistically important of the
Ecuadorian cultures is that associated with La Tolita. Many of its
pottery figurines seem to be associated with Mexican art styles,
but they now prove to be earlier in time. The Ecuadorian period is
from 500 BC to 500 AD. It looked at one time as if the Mexican
legend of the departure south of some tribes who later returned to
become ancestors of the Toltecs referred to this location in the far
south. The La Tolita figurines have large heads and realistically
modelled bodies, often of considerable beauty. Women wear
skirts to the ankles, men sometimes wear a loincloth, but mostly

they seem to take pride in displaying their penis. Jewellery was worn on legs, arms, neck, nose and ears, and the bodies are marked often by lines, but whether this means tattoo or paint is not clear. It is possible that the figures represent real people since they are shown in pairs and even taking sexual pleasure from each other. Some may be deities or perhaps great noblemen. But there are also figurines of monstrous creatures wearing elaborately decorated jaguar heads. Others can only be described as wearing formalized monster heads. Presumably these are creatures of the earth magic type. A few stone figures of the region also show human and animal characteristics mixed. Golden animal figurines and small golden masks are fairly common, and a few of the figurines wear earrings and nose-moons of gold. Most implements seem to have been made of wood and stone, and there is a great variety of axe-blades made from fine hard stone. They show many differing forms apparently suited to different uses.

In this millennium after 500 BC, there were some seven or eight differing cultures active in western Ecuador, all producing fine pottery, all using gold, all casting copper and various types of bronze. Basically they were all farming communities, but of their villages there are only a few earthen mounds to mark sites. Presumably they traded with each other as well as fought, but they have left no form of historical record. There are great stone slabs with figures in relief, but they seem to be memorials of events which were probably recorded by verbal histories. Nothing remains from which we could construct a history of the people. Even the names are but place names of typical sites. What we have is a great variety of pottery types showing persistent differences and thus illustrating the tribal divisions of the time.

Just as there was a sudden change of culture in about 500 BC, there is another break about 500 AD. The archaeologists give us dates which are all very similar. The multiplicity of tribal styles gives way to a greater simplicity, and three cultural types remain only on the west coast. What occasioned the change we do not know. It was possibly a matter of inter-tribal wars, but some great passion for migration might have obsessed the people. Even a pestilence might have altered the balance of things, but we simply have no evidence. On the sites of the older La Tolita culture, we find that the Manteño culture takes over.

There is a slight continuity of basic forms, but a greater ability in sculpture brings in larger figures. Stone platforms for buildings are made and a number of stone seats which represent a crouching figure supporting the seat on its back. They seem to have represented the rising status of local chiefs. An important relic from this last phase of coastal architecture is two wooden houseposts, now in the Museum at Guayaquil. They have been carved with pairs of male and female figures and some alligators. They at least prove that wooden architecture was not a matter of posts and lintels without decoration. It may possibly be that the amalgamation of coastal cultures represented developments in-land in which the tribes around Quito were united under the rule of the Scyri.

The central rule of the Scyri of Quito was strong, and the typical heavy ceramics and fine bronze work show the range of his authority. Towards the end of independence we find that the Ecuadorian peoples were copying Inca-style pottery, though much more coarsely and with little masks and bits of modelling which would have scandalized Inca purists. They constructed some roads, probably because the Inca invention had practical uses. They even made fortresses on the southern pattern, with rings of great stones holding fighting platforms from which warriors armed with lances and slings could resist attack. The Scyri knew, of course, about the rise of Inca power and the remarkable military conquests of his southern neighbour. Whether he believed in the Inca contention that they were making a new world of Four Quarters dedicated to the sun and the advancement of the human race, we do not know. The very fact of the existence of Quito as a strong power to the north of Peru was sufficient incentive for its conquest. The Incas really believed that they were commissioned to unify the world. To take Quito was necessary before extension of their benign rule into the northern Andes.

After the usual formalities, Huayna Ccapac came with his immense armies with their spears and darts, and regiments all in similar coloured tunics. Their copper helmets glittered under the sun. The battles were quite easy defeats of the soldiers of Quito in their fortresses. They were simply surrounded by a sea of warriors, subjected to a beating with sling stones and then told to surrender, which they usually did. There was no way in which Quito could be defended, and so the last independent ruler in Ecuador lost his throne, except that he was made a privileged vassal of the Inca.

As has happened in history so often, a pair of beautiful eyes altered human history. They belonged to one of the many princesses born to the Scyri by his many wives. She was desirable beyond even the great wealth in gold that had been taken from Quito. So the elderly Inca took her as one of his wives. All his wives, however, were subject to his sister-wife, whose son Huascar must inherit the empire. But the love of Huayna Ccapac and the Quitan Princess was deep indeed. When she bore him a

Standing figure of a jaguar deity, from Costa Rica, 10th or 11th century AD.

Staff end: a golden pelican, from Panama, c. 12th century AD.

son, the Emperor was filled with happiness. He decreed in his stupid joy that the young Prince Atahuallpa should inherit Quito and part of Peru, that the boy should inherit equally with the true heir, the Son of the Sun through both mother and father. This was sheer treason against his father the sun god, Inti. But Huayna Ccapac appears to have taken no notice of tradition.

When the young princes were grown men, their father died. Naturally the princes called their followers and began a struggle for power. Atahuallpa had two highly skilled Quitan generals to aid him, and after a campaign right through Peru he captured and imprisoned the true Son of the Sun. Peru was shattered by this turn of events. Then the white sailed ships from Panama arrived bringing Pizarro. For nine months the Spaniards rode along the Peruvian coasts and took over towns without any opposition. Then came the battle, and Atahuallpa, having ordered the murder of his imprisoned brother, was himself made captive. Through Colombia and Ecuador Spanish soldiers marched southwards to assist in the defeat of the Incas and to share in the plunder of Peru. The world of the American Indians was at an end.

But before we abandon it, we must find out how Peru came into being and what developed there through the ages.

6 The Peruvian Development

AS WE HAVE SEEN, VILLAGE CULTURES SOON DEVELOPED in Peru both in the highlands and along the coast. The great highland culture of Chavin soon spread to the north coast as the Cupisnique culture. However, by the third century BC great changes were on their way, at least as far as art-work was concerned. Ceramic forms rapidly become more elegant, and decorative techniques alter, for example, in the south coast from the post-firing application of resin-based colours to the use of coloured slips for polychrome pottery. In weaving the over-all embroidery techniques continue but they are accompanied by tapestry and damask techniques, tie-dyeing appears and the kelim weaves with slits at the borders of colour areas develops. Gauze had appeared earlier. The early use of gold develops a new richness of design, and silver and bronze appear. There is also a change in burial techniques: the early bodies laid out on a matting bier are replaced by mummy bundles wrapped up in great quantities of clothes.

On the northern coast, where buildings were made of adobe, there were radical developments in building styles. The rolls of adobe were replaced by walls built of alternating clay cones, but this changed fairly soon to more solid constructions of brick-like masses of adobe. Altogether there was a considerable development based on the past but stepping forward into what must be called civilization, based on small towns and a type of centralized government.

On both the northern and the southern halves of the Peruvian coast pottery vessels show humans in a way which indicates that a definite class system had evolved, which includes lords, warriors and people of little account. There are also many strange beings, usually with tusked mouths which indicate their superhuman ferocity and power. Although the two areas are widely divergent in almost all aspects of culture, their gods seem to be very closely related to the divine beings of the Chavín culture. It is clear that this basic religion of Peru was concerned with the powers of nature. It reminds one of the later popular religion in Inca times

Pottery portrait of a Mochica warrior wearing face paint, from Peru, 4th or 5th century AD.

173

when everything unusual was thought to be inhabited by a spirit power. From pots we are clear that mountain peaks, the maize ears, the sea beasts, foxes and deer, as well as a bearded god very like the later concept of the bringer of civilization, Viracocha, were all worshipped. There are strange bean-men on the northern coasts, perhaps vegetation spirits, and in the south we find many paintings of such fertility spirits.

We have very little information about the astronomical side of religion, except that in the southern area there are the mysterious linear constructions on the hill tops behind the site of Nasca. Here there are a number of straight alignments of smallish white or cream stones. They are long lines, sometimes more than a kilometre in length. They are straight, but the directions are not all on one alignment. There are sets which vary by seven or eight degrees. Across the lines there are huge outline pictures of birds. Now these lines and pictures cannot be seen as such from the ground. The lines may indeed be sighting lines for astronomical objects, and so their direction alone is important. The birds are exactly like birds on textiles of the Nasca culture, of the early centuries BC or AD. They could have been set out from a woven pattern in which each stitch is equated with one pace. The scale would be about right. But why make birds by pacing out a design which makes no sense from the ground? It is suggested that the lines were landing marks for 'flying saucers', but then the textile-design birds would have little meaning. More likely the straight lines are sighting lines for local priestly astronomers, and the gigantic birds are symbols for some of the planets. One does not imagine that the Nasca people were aviators, but the birds are far less visible from the ground than the hill figures of southern England. They are distant cousins of the linear birds of Chavín sculpture, but instead of great vultures, they are mostly innocent humming-birds. This is appropriate enough for representing the slow progress of the planets among the stars of night.

This southern culture, centred around the Nasca valley and the Paracas peninsula, was spiritually very close to the Chavín culture. Its gods were probably the same, but technically it advanced all the arts. Ceramics become all-over polychrome, and textiles which begin with over-all embroidery on a plain web are turned into woven tapestries of many technical processes. Decorations on bone and wood all echo the local styles, and stonework is there, but still simple. There is much evidence about house building techniques from various valleys for although this civilization flowered in a grim desert region where a few posts supporting a textile covering was the ideal, there were large settlements at Cahvachi, Tambo Viejo and Dos Palmas.

Pot decorated with animal motifs, from Nasca.

Pottery vessel showing seated woman with speckled dress, from Nasca, Peru, 4th or 5th century AD.

The textiles from the Paracas peninsula are astounding. They are large; in many cases as much as seven metres in length and five in width. Such great sheets were used to cover bundles made up of layers of clothing around crouching dried bodies. At first they were covered with all-over embroidery, but later tapestry and kelim weaves are found. The themes are mostly religious, though some decorative linear patterns are found. The forms shown are usually animal. Jaguar, condor and serpent predominate, and human figures often wear animal masks and carry serpents. Some of them are flying, and many have sharp animal claws. No doubt they are gods of dreadful powers. Many carry human heads at their girdle or in their hands, and most carry long spear-throwers and war clubs. The whole aspect is one of a brave Red Indian warrior cult in which head-taking was important.

Pottery carries the theme still further. The ceramics are of a

Globular pottery vessel painted with a bird stealing beans, from Nasca, 2nd or 3rd century AD.

well baked red ware covered with polychrome painting. The potters had great skills in deciding what colouring mixtures were to be used on the slips. When painted on, they appeared as faintly tinted whites, and only after firing was the final rich colour revealed. So finely were the pots burnished that the smooth surfaces shine in the light. Many of the pots are painted with pastoral themes; gods of beans and squash work in the fields; birds are painted with loving care, and these include pretty little finches as well as the larger birds. Serpents appear, and in many cases dragons or heavenly serpents are shown. The gods also fly through the air carrying trophy heads. Some pots show rows of heads, and single-head pots show that the heads were dried and the mouth sewn up. In fact the graves have yielded up such human heads, not shrunken because the skull is retained. They were fitted with a string loop through the occiput for fastening.

The polychrome pots from Nasca are among the most beautiful art works of the Americas and show that this was a high civilization in which specialist artists could be employed as potters and weavers in a rich metal-using society.

Food was largely maize, with ground nuts, beans of several kinds, llama meat and a great deal of fish. The potters were experts in painting fish in dishes, as all potters of all times have been tempted to depict. The fishermen went to sea in small boats of bundles of reeds like those used today on Lake Titicaca far inland. They used nets and copper fish-hooks.

The emphasis on food is much more about the sea among the northern Mochica; and among the Nasca folk to the south vegetation and birds are more important. There is no reason to think that the Nasca people were bad fishermen: they had to rely very largely on the myriads of fish in the northward current along the coast, but apart from the potters' conventional design of fishes on dishes, there is little in Nasca art to show the importance of sea food in their dietary. Again there was a truly American Indian streak about them, for their pots, as well as occasional real examples, testify that they were head-hunters. But there is no evidence of cannibalism, though for some of their tools they used human as well as llama bones. Many pots have pictures of warriors carrying staves with copper axe blades set in them, and most men wore head-dresses with slings coiled around them. One imagines them as a basically peaceful farming community deeply interested in the natural world around them but also constantly involved in frontier wars either to defend themselves or to conquer new farmlands.

Agriculture was conducted in both areas of the coast with much ceremony. There were planting and harvest festivals. As the coastal region was a grim desert, the river valleys which irrigated narrow areas were precious to the people. In many cases there was a little irrigation practised by digging canals which spread the river water over larger areas. So the land was watered, and many ceremonies were made to increase its fertility. We find fertility gods on the pottery of the region. In the south around Nasca one finds pictures of plants, and many have depictions of curious beings walking among the crops. They often have animal heads, or even take the total form of animals. They guard principally the various kinds of bean, and walk menacingly as they guard the life of the crops. Sometimes such creatures appear on textiles, and quite often they carry the heads of human victims as an indication of their great ferocity. It is rare among the Nasca people to find representations of fertility ceremonies or of sex, though there are in the later period a few vases in the form of

Pottery vessel showing man wearing typical hat and shirt decorated with llama heads, from Tiahuanaco, between 700 and 900 AD.

OVERLEAF, LEFT Three Mochica pottery vessels with realistic faces: a flute-player; a potter modelling a vase; and a fully armed warrior, between 5th and 7th centuries AD.

OVERLEAF, RIGHT Woven textile with pattern of faces showing eyes and teeth; above each eye a small coloured cap, Tiahuanaco culture, between 500 and 900 AD.

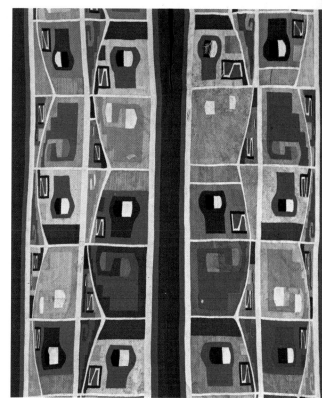

Featherwork 'breastplate' with the figure of a Chimu god and shell bead pendants, 13th or 14th century AD.

naked girls displaying their sex organs with symbolic patterns on them.

In the Museum at Lima a lay figure of an Indian is dressed in the full equipment of clothing from a Paracas grave. It is dignified and splendid, with a long tunic and waistband, a great embroidered cape and an attractive sash worn as a turban. The whole effect is of a civilized man from a centre of high culture. Indeed we must regard the Nasca culture as a civilization of note and as one of the most perfect descendants of the Chavín culture of a thousand years earlier. The Nasca culture survived for some five or six centuries into the Christian era, showing some stylistic advances in pottery and a steady increase in the amount of textile made, though the large embroidered sheets disappeared. Some new pottery forms were made in the later days, many of them representing realistic animals and fruit. Several of these were fitted with whistles consisting of a hollow ceramic ball across the lip of which the act of pouring water brought in a blast of air and produced a whistling chirrup.

We find a few vases representing people, and some wear copper helmets, but it is quite unclear whether any represent chiefs. In fact there is such a confusion in the human figures on textiles as well as pottery that one cannot tell which is human and which divine. The textile figures often include great masks of gods of which the features are tiny human types. There are also among the early embroidered textiles many divine figures in which the conventional personage wears a mask with golden whiskers like a divine cat. Often the cat form extends as a garment down the back and ends with a ringed tail. Such figures carry their typical long war club with its copper blade and also human heads in the hand or pendant from the belt. Some figures wear garments fringed with human heads. Since the Nasca people could not shrink heads, these divine terrors were obviously thought of as giants. Many different face paints are worn, but the cat mask, known archaeologically to be really a huge nose clip, is almost universal. It seems to have been an important symbol of chiefly rank. Presumably the indication is that their war god was a gigantic puma, no doubt descended from the puma deities found at Chavín and other early highland sites.

An interesting feature of Peru in the centuries around the beginning of the Christian era was the wide difference between two major coastal cultures. The northern part of the coast, especially around the Lambayeque and Casma valleys, was once the centre of the Cupisnique culture, but as time went on, the ceramic styles changed radically. Vases still retained the looped spouts, called stirrup spouts, but they became thinner, and the

bodies became more globular. The old heavy black ware gave way
to a fine redware, very thin and tempered with sand. Often the
vases were made in sections which were moulded by pouring
plastic clay into a waxed pottery mould and swishing it around
until the slip hardened and could be tilted out of the mould. Then
the sections of the pot were assembled, the edges wetted and luted
together with a little soft clay. In this way many delicate forms
could be made. The spouts and loop pouring ducts became
thinner and more delicate. The basic colours of the pots at first
were white patterns painted on the red bodies. They became
painted all over with white slip and then decorated with red-
painted designs. It appears that the dry pots were fired in an open
heap of brushwood. Many bear burn marks, and no trace of any
kiln has been found in the area.

The culture which produced this remarkable pottery was
named Mochica, because the natives of that part of Peru at the
time of the Conquest spoke the Muchik language, but in
accordance with modern custom in which cultural phases are
named from a type site or place the Mochica culture has been
neatly, and accurately, named from the valley of Moche. There
the whole series of pots and textiles of the culture have been
found, so the old name is still meaningful. One supposes that the
culture is derived from the older Chavín-Cupisnique since there
are intermediate stages, but the final product is utterly unlike the
early stages. Apparently some of the gods survived the changes
since many of the later figures of gods wear grimacing masks with
great fangs which remind one of heads from Chavín. Sometimes
one finds vases with images of warriors tying on their head-
dresses over what appears to be a god-mask so that they would
present a more terrifying appearance to the enemy. Others wear
masks in the form of foxes, pumas, owls and other birds. We have
no knowledge of the names of the gods, but their functions are
usually clear from the paintings. However, they do not include
the number of vegetation deities which we find in the Nasca
culture. A few pictures show war, with clubs and slings, but there
seems to have been little head-hunting, though prisoners seem to
have been treated with cruelty. Often we find painted figures of
running warriors and perhaps spirit beings, who carry little bags
in their hands. It is thought that they contained speckled beans
which conveyed messages; but it is equally likely that they were
sachets of dried and crushed coca leaves. This stimulant and
pain-killer was used in Peru from early times since it is found in
bags in graves of many periods.

We know little of Mochica domestic architecture. Small towns
were built, and adobes of clay were used for building, in the early

Heavily embroidered gauze shirt from Pachacamac, central Peru, *c.* 800–900 AD.

periods of conical shape but later squarish slabs were used. The small houses had open roofs which were covered with awnings in that hot rainless region. The great works were enormous adobe pyramids which once housed little buildings on top containing sacred images. Although the winds have done some damage to the adobe constructions, the pyramidal mounds remain as impressively massive structures dominating the regions around. Some of these great pyramids originated before the full development of the Mochica culture, in the preliminary culture which we know as Salinar. But they continued in use in the Mochica period and no doubt were centres of an educated priesthood who organized the ceremonies of the people. There are no buildings which we should call palaces, and it may be that the culture was

Pair of Mochica golden ear ornaments with figures of a sky god, 7th or 8th century AD.

organized on the basis of a High Chief who was also a High Priest. We cannot, of course, be certain. Many civilizations followed that path, but again many had a dual control in which the religious chief delegated full powers to a war leader in times of emergency. In a non-historical world, dependent on archaeological discovery, we have no very decisive data. We note, however, that in Mochica art there are personages sitting on thrones and people carried in litters. They are obviously nobles of importance and are given ceremonial treatment which is similar to that given to the gods.

There was social differentiation within the culture. There is a pot in the British Museum which shows a weaving workshop in which a large lady is in charge of a weaving shed where a number of less important women are busy weaving. Each one has a water bottle and a supply of tapestry-needles. Also each one has a pattern of cloth hanging beside her loom. They are obviously weaving garments in an organized production unit, and they owe obedience to the large lady. There were probably several such weaving sheds in any Mochica town, and they produced garments for the living as well as for grave wear.

There was, no doubt, a great reliance in ancient Peru on astronomy. The position of the stars marked a calendar for the people on earth. The slow progression of the heavens around the southern pole led by the remarkable star group of the Southern Cross must have been important to all farmers, since the position of the stars marked the seasons. But everywhere the moon was the most important time marker. We find representations of moon-like creatures in both cultures, but they are much clearer from the

Mochica people of the north coast. They worshipped the moon as more important than the sun, and presumably they managed a method of adjusting the length of their year to the sequence of the moons. The position of new moon in the solar year recurs only about once in nineteen years, the Greek *saros*, so there had to be a continuous cyclic adjustment each year so that the solar calendar should truly reflect the seasons. The farmers had to know the solar day on which it was best to plant beans and maize; the magicians had to know all about the position of the moon. Thus there must have been a constant adjustment to meet secular and religious needs within the community. Probably they knew enough to predict eclipses, but apart from knowing of the ceremonies in later times to drive the devouring shadow from the sun, it is not clear from our archaeological material how the event was calculated or what it was supposed to mean as a symbol of events yet to come.

There are many paintings on the pots of warriors dressed in thick loincloths and tunics either fighting or running in a kind of procession in which they carry small bags, perhaps of coca leaves. It seems as if a great deal of ceremonial importance was attached to this armed race.

Great chiefs are shown seated upon stepped thrones, and they are obviously seen as akin to the gods. Probably they were semi-divine beings because of their office. But the real gods are shown with canine fangs and look very ferocious indeed. These gods sometimes emerge from the sea as monstrous crabs, or dragons, a few are snail like, but the human manifestations wear a curious head-dress rather like a Napoleonic hat. It appears to have been a badge of great importance. Maybe it was originally derived from some kind of seashell. But the sea and all its creatures are shown as beings of primary importance to the Mochica. In a few vases the sea is represented by a wavy line of which the crests are shown as animal heads. It was a living entity from which all life seems to emerge and upon which the Mochica fishermen in their reed-bundle boats set out to earn their living. The head of the Mochica dragon is really that of a sea lion showing its teeth. This, combined with the pictures of sea lion hunters, leads one to suppose that the sea lion was also a divine animal, perhaps an image of the destructive power of the ocean.

Sometimes we find pots painted with great reed boats, on which small bands of warriors engage in combat. These boats often have the dragon head as a prow ornament. The warriors swing their huge clubs at one another and a few use slings. There is so much decoration on these pots that it seems as if the fighting scenes illustrated an old legend.

Mochica wood carving is of excellent quality. Wood was used for making the dreadful clubs shown in the vase paintings. The head was a flanged dome, and the stem tapered down to a point. The weapon was swung to break an enemy's head, and then if necessary the warrior reversed it and used the point to pierce his victim's skull. Other warriors carried bronze hand axes. These objects were pierced at the blunt end so that they could be hung on the hand by a stout string loop. The heavy axe blade was used for crushing and scarring the enemy. Slings were also used and often worn twined around the head. The defence against these weapons was a small shield either circular about twenty inches in diameter or square, which was fringed with a series of strong cords used to entrap flying shafts. The warriors usually wore cotton tunics heavily quilted, and they protected their heads with thick rolls of cotton cloth, though in a minority of cases metal helmets were worn. It appears that many of the greater nobles wore thick turbans to which a wooden mask was attached, usually of some frightening animal, though sometimes they represented bird heads.

We are not well acquainted with the gods of the Mochica people. There is a very fierce male being with great canine teeth, who is otherwise a man. He seems to be a powerful deity. There is also an owl-faced deity and several creatures with bird heads which may be planetary beings. Important in the series are the wooden figures, dug up a century ago from under sixty feet of guano, in the Chincha Islands. These represent a male god wearing the sacred head-dress rather like a Napoleonic hat, and several figures of a seated naked man. This last is apparently the Evening Star. A legend recorded in the sixteenth century tells us that once the Evening Star came up from the sea. He made love to the two wives of a great chief and had pleasant intercourse. When the husband came home and found this wild play going on, he had the malefactor tied up and cast into the western ocean. So the prisoner figures probably portray the ending of this legend. In some cases the confining rope ends in a sea lion head biting the glans penis of the prisoner. Although these wooden figures were excavated from under some sixty feet depth of guano, there is no reason to think that they were earlier than the second or first century BC.

The Mochica seem to have lived in towns much smaller than the great urban areas of their successors, the Chimú. Some of the pottery vessels show small houses with a canopied extension on the roof. Roofs are often decorated with war clubs as if the clubs were stuck into the thatch. Maybe this showed that the house was the home of a military man of importance.

Apparently many people went in for body decoration, and

Mochica head of wooden staff inlaid with mother-of-pearl showing jaguar deity copulating with a woman, from Peru, between 2nd century BC and 3rd or 4th century AD.

some of the mummies have tattoo designs in dark blue on forearms and faces. The overall mask-like painting of the Nasca peoples was not used, but a row of small decorative elements across chin and forehead are known from pots, and a few of the figure vases show faces painted half red and half white on the left and right, but this was not an important pattern since it is rare. Mochica warriors also painted black patterns on their legs to resemble socks to mid-calf level, and most of them also painted a black disc over the knee cap. A few feminine figures show a little tattoo across the chin, but this is rare. Both men and women pierced their ears and stretched the lobe to accommodate huge circular flares which were held in position by a pin thrust through the back. Some specimens excavated from graves are beautiful works based on wood, inlaid with turquoise and copper carbonate and with sheet gold decoration. Men trimmed their hair across the forehead, but women parted theirs and drew it back.

The development of portraiture in the form of pottery heads is unique in the arts of America and rare enough in the world. Its emergence in the third to sixth centuries AD probably reflects a cult which demanded the preservation of a realistic likeness of the deceased, as it was in Roman society. They are comparatively few in number, so this superb art was probably reserved to members of the ruling classes. Among the portrait heads we find that a few women are included, evidence that they held an important position in society, and some of the male heads show marks of war and disease. One head shows a one-eyed man, and several show neatly trimmed areas of the lower nose and upper lips, which are probably evidence of the disease Leishmaniasis which destroys these tissues. It appears as if surgery has been employed to clean up the diseased areas.

When Mochica and Nasca cultures were fully developed, influences begin to appear of a new art style from the highlands. This new influence seems to have come from two contemporary centres, a southern one from Tiahuanaco, beside Lake Titicaca, and a northern one from Huari. There are differences in detail between the two styles, but the similarities are so great that it may well be that Tiahuanaco was the religious heart of a civilization administered from Huari. The penetration of the coastal regions occurred in the late eighth and the ninth century AD. There are no historical records of this expansion. It was particularly thorough in the south, where the Nasca culture at first repeated Tia-huanacoid art and then disappeared for ever, leaving the coast to be populated only by small villages of fisher folk. In the north the Mochica culture was influenced, and it tended to accept designs based on the arts of Huari. Pottery becomes much less elaborate

Chimu golden plate showing vegetation goddess and planting ceremonies, possibly a calendar, 12th or 13th century AD.

and reflects some forms of the highland ceramics, including a few heads of a typically Tiahuanaco aspect, rather broad strong faces wearing small vertical caps. In weaving too we find that the growth of strange designs from the highland culture nearly supersedes the local styles: a velvet technique was used for hats. But the eclipse of culture is not so complete as it was in the Nasca area to the south. However, it looks as if the mainspring of Mochica inspiration was broken, and the living art of that culture was lost. It may well be that the people of the Huari culture took ships to investigate the Pacific, for a kneeling stone figure very reminiscent of this culture was found on Easter Island. It is earlier than the great Polynesian Moai of the island and may represent the work of a previous invasion from the east. Similarly late Mochica pottery was found on the Galapagos as well as fourteenth-century black ware. This indicates that there were probably two periods of naval exploration from Peru. The pottery was not in great quantity and may represent debris from a couple of trading rafts sailing northwards from Peru.

Huari is a much ruined site in the Andes with quantities of the typical pottery. Tiahuanaco has long been famous for its ancient ruins of temple walls, sunken courtyards and the Gate of the Sun. Pottery includes large figures of llamas with burdens and a number of ceremonial beakers (*kero*) painted with formalized heads of pumas and eagles. Sometimes the head is modelled in a cubic form on the lip of the vessel. There is a number of head vases all wearing upright caps and all rather grim in expression. They give the impression of being men of a dominant and unpitying power. The extent to which they imposed their ideas of design on the coastal peoples indicates an imperial power not unlike that of the later Incas. In the textiles we find designs based on animal heads and birds, all of a strongly conventionalized angular design as if drawn out on squared paper. Sometimes we find a human head design, always wearing a high cap and often distorted into narrow strips in which one can just identify the elements of the design. It is usual for the head to have a tear dropping from the eye, and this may link it with the sun god, the figure on the gateway at Tiahuanaco. This figure at Tiahuanaco presents some interesting artistic problems. Several features in the centre seem to be direct descendants from the Chavín culture. The figure itself, with the weeping eyes, is probably the sun, who according to an Inca legend wept tears of gold upon the earth. It may well represent Viracocha, the creator, to whom a similar legend was attached. All around the central figure are rows of kneeling winged figures with Condor and Puma masks. Perhaps the whole concept is related to the idea of the sun among the moving ranks of stars, but

The ruins of Machupicchu, the Inca fortified city.

Pottery vase with head of man with face paint, Tiahuanaco style, early 10th century AD.

Stone figure of a squatting man from Pokotia, Tiahuanaco, Bolivia, 8th or 9th century AD.

there is no literary evidence by which we could confirm this. The gateway stands in its true historical position between the arts of Chavín and the Incas. Whether it confirms the post-Conquest story by Montesinos that the Incas were descended from a line of four hundred Amautas who ruled at Tiahuanaco is not very clear. In any case the number four hundred is not probable.

The Tiahuanaco style in free-standing sculptures is of monolithic blocks of which each of the four faces presents a rendering of the figure in all its cubic conformation. In Huari the stone figures are slightly more naturalistic. The figures at Tiahuanaco are free standing but they formed parts of a colonnade around vast sunken courtyards and ruined walls. In Inca times Tiahuanaco was described as the place where Viracocha emerged to create the world. It was a sacred spot to the Incas. A pair of wonderful embroidered shirts which must have belonged to an Inca of the highest degree, possibly the Supreme Inca himself, were found in a stone chest in the palace among the ruins.

But all is uncertainty. Tiahuanaco and Huari had fallen and were deserted by most of the population probably in the tenth century AD at a period when Peruvian culture was at a low ebb. There seems to have been a great deal of disruption of civilization. Old boundaries are overrun, and many minor cultures developed both on the coasts and in the highlands.

The north seems to have been the country from which much of the disruption occurred. It had always been an area of culture contact, and its influence seems to have been responsible for the introduction of pottery in Peru. In the early centuries AD it produced a culture area around Recuay which is remarkable for a ceramic series different from any other Peruvian style. The bodies of the pots are coiled and have a matt surface of pinkish clay. On this are painted patterns in white and black. Very often the top of the vessel is closed by a group of clay structures representing people and buildings. Sometimes there are two layers in which the figures vary in size, the largest representing gods to whom offerings are made. All the figures wear long tunics, and the headdress is a cap with projecting pleating at either side. Buildings seem to consist of a square room with a roof and canopy. A remarkable aspect of Recuay pottery is that much use is made of a wax-resist technique when painting pots. This is much more characteristic of Colombia than of Peru. It may be an indication that the people of Recuay had moved in from the northern mountains. The culture lasted for a few centuries before it was overwhelmed by Huari.

One can see from the foregoing that life in Peru developed steadily and then became static. The last millennium BC was a period of great advancement. City states developed, navigation of a simple kind ended in a routine of trade along the coasts. The arts of weaving developed an ever-increasing complexity of work. Pottery became an industry of great technical skill. The use of metals grew into the verge of a bronze age. The social structure included divine chiefs and a three-tier grouping of people into lords, citizens and slaves. Technology was entirely by hand, but workshops were being developed. Clothing was elaborate, and insignia of rank were worn in the form of specially woven cloth and fine ornaments. Thus, by the beginning of the Christian era, we can say that Peru consisted of at least three major states with some areas of minor cultures between them. Great pyramids had been built along the coast, and some of the regions had developed marked roadways, both on the sandy coasts and up in the Andes. Their main purpose was for trade but also they made possible rapid movements of armies. The llama was a beast of burden, domesticated and used in huge convoys of hundreds of animals. Towns were built in adobe brick on the coast, and large stone built villages were made in the highlands. Religion was a worship of the creator and the powers of nature, often terrifying.

The first millennium AD was a period of consolidation. Technology was refined and somewhat more diversified. Golden ornaments, together with silver and turquoise, developed a greater splendour. Clothing was but little altered, and although the over-all embroidered textiles disappeared, the more complex forms of hand-weaving replaced them. Growing civilization brought problems of defence with it; so we find an increase in the numbers of defensive fortresses usually in the shape of natural rocky mounds refaced with adobe brick to present a number of fighting stages up which an enemy must climb in face of slings and spears.

The major advance in this period seems to have been in the field of government. The powerful states of the Mochica and Nasca people were large unities, ruled from small cities. There was obviously a careful state organization behind these nations, and the ruling classes were very splendidly decorated. It may be that these states were theocracies, and their splendid temples indicate that there must have been a priestly class closely linked with the secular organization.

Towards the end of the period we find that the highland peoples from Tiahuanaco in the south and Huari in the north had overrun and subverted the coastal cultures. The Mochica culture survived the assault, but the latest Mochica work is very poor and lacks the living impulse of the earlier works. Elsewhere the domination seems to have been complete. The great temples

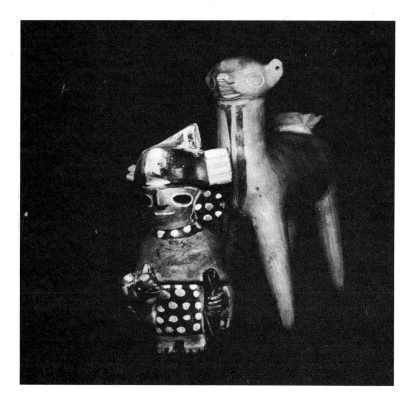

Pottery figure of man leading llama and carrying llama foal, from Recuay, central Peru, *c.* 800 AD or earlier.

remained in use, probably because the religion of the conquerors was not greatly different from the earliest religions of the region, which in turn had inspired the beliefs of the coastal people. The cause of this great resurgence of the mountain cultures is unknown to us. It may have been due to a dominating warrior class or even have been an echo of a population explosion. We have no traditions surviving, and since the Peruvians had no system of written history, we are left with facts without an explanation. It is an interesting speculation that the breakdown might have been due to a climatic change, since it is nearly contemporary with the Maya breakdown in the early tenth century. But so far we have no good explanation of the sudden rise of the Andean cultures or of the catastrophic collapse a couple of centuries later.

The invasion and collapse of Tiahuanaco and Huari changed life on the southern coast of Peru for the next centuries. The tribes of the highlands seem to have spent a great deal of time in fortifying their villages, as if there was a period of civil war and great uncertainty about the political circumstances. On the northern coast the debased remnants of the Mochica culture continued for a while. But the picture of Peru at the beginning of the eleventh century is one of an impoverished country of varying population clusters awaiting a new inspiration.

7 The Divine Rulers

PERU IN THE ELEVENTH CENTURY WAS A LAND OF MANY small cultures, all of them poor and possibly with a small population. There were echoes of previous cultures but nothing of great importance. All the achievements of the previous periods of high culture were available to the people. The food plants, weaving, pottery and metal were all in full use. But the divided state of the country held back any advancement.

City states were very small in the mountains, and the towns were less important than the countryside where food was hunted on the desolate *punas*, and grain cultivated in river valleys and on hillside terraces. All towns built a fortress of staged ramparts of earth faced with stone.

Somewhere about the end of the century, according to Inca legend, an odd event took place. First a small group of three men and a woman came into the mountains. Their descendants said they came from the terrible forests of the Amazon basin; one wonders if they actually came from a town where they had access to the roadway which ran along the heavily wooded foothills of the eastern flank of the Andes. This small group came up to the mountains above Cuzco, claiming that they carried a wedge of gold which had been entrusted to them by their father, the sun. They had been told that each time they camped, the wedge was to be laid on the ground. When their future centre was found, the wedge would sink into the earth. The sister left her three brothers and hunted down a llama. She cut it open and removed the lungs. The windpipe was in her mouth. She blew into it and it swelled up all red and bloody. Then, with one of her brothers, she went down to Cuzco. The other two brothers, by a great magic, were turned into sacred rocks. As she came to Cuzco, the people fled at the terrible sight. Then she and her brother seized a small house and became the rulers of the lower half of Cuzco. Thus came the Incas into their inheritance, for on that very night the golden wedge sank into the ground and was never seen again. One of the other brothers became the rock Hanacauri, and the other became the great animal-formed Kenko stone. For three generations of

Chimu blackware vase showing the god Aiapaiec struggling with a seadragon, 12th or 13th century AD.

brother-sister marriage, the Inca family did not move. They remained only rulers of lower Cuzco, though their pretensions were great.

This fantastic story is the beginning of history in Peru. The events took place at about 1100 AD. The main thing to note is that the Inca family was but one among many groups of rulers of tribes and small towns in the mountains. They were not unique in fact, though their claim to be children of the sun was probably unique in the totality of that statement. It involved the continuous marriage of eldest brother and eldest sister in the family so that the pure line of descent from the sun was preserved. This was their patent of nobility, and it must never be broken.

In the lowlands of the coast the smaller towns after the collapse in the tenth century were slowly moving into groups. The southern half of the coast never united, but it is believed that part of it became a state called Chincha, of which the pottery covered with textile-derived patterns is known as Ica style, from the town site and river valley in which it was first identified. Further to the north was the state of Cuismancu. This area has yielded some fine textiles and the remarkable Chancay pottery. This ware is rough, sandy in texture and colour, painted with linear designs in a blue-black tone reminiscent of manganese colour. The forms of great melon-shaped vases and rather clumsy standing figures, all naked, are smooth and attractive. Nevertheless, it is clear that the Cuismancu technicians had not reached the standards of their ancestors.

The lands of the Mochica people were invaded by strangers who came from the sea on large balsa rafts sailing from the north. These were the courtiers and servants of Taycanamo, the culture hero of the Chimú people, as he is called in later writings. The Chimú people were great metal workers, producing fine vessels in gold and silver and even able to weld copper, which is a very difficult process. To accomplish this, the artificers must have laid the copper in a bed of finely ground charcoal, exposing only a tiny area at a time for welding. Thus we see a people of great skill, settling in the river valleys and starting up a kingdom from a beautiful walled city known as Chan Chan. They were nearly contemporary with the emergence of the Incas. The Chimú kingdom eventually absorbed an independent northern group who had continued the old Mochica culture, though in a sadly debased state. But this tradition influenced Chimú art to the greater artistic development of ceramic forms. Some beautiful animal vases in the Chimú blackware testify to this Mochica strain surviving in the Chimú kingdom.

The first of the Chimú gods was called Aiapaec and goes back to Mochica times. He is shown on the vases and wood carvings as a man with a tusked face, strongly reminiscent of the early Chavín works. The general air of ferocity of this being makes one feel that he was representative of the terrible powers of nature. The great sky spirit was the divine Sí, the moon. This race of fishermen preferred the cool moonlit evenings to the dreadful heat of the sunny days on their desert coast. The powers of the natural world were very important to the Chimú, and we find that the rainbow was a sacred symbol, made rather like a millipede in form. Their decorative art is covered with animals – sea lions, fish, pelicans, and monkeys – in great profusion. One feels that these creatures were in some way holy things, as well as the sources of food for mankind. One textile shows a sea deity in the midst of sea creatures, as a symbol of the gift of life.

It appears that the Chimú utilized the old adobe pyramids in their area of Peru as temples and built only a few additions to them. On their southern borders they built an enormous terraced fortress in the Fortaleza valley. There are several Chimú towns, testifying to a great growth of population in the twelfth and thirteenth centuries. The capital city of Chan Chan was a grouping of ten enormous walled courtyards. Each surround was forty or fifty feet in height and built of adobe brick or else cast in great slabs of adobe moulded with patterns of birds and beasts with gods and rainbows all in the style of the local textiles. The walls were plastered and decorated with highly coloured friezes in relief. These coastal cities must have been remarkably beautiful. In areas between the compounds there were spaces used for burial grounds and possibly meeting places. The town was built on sandy desert and rocky areas not suitable for agriculture, but each great compound included a garden where the earth had been excavated down to the water-table. Here grew food plants and flowers. Around were small temple pyramids, houses for the chiefs and lodgings for their retinue. All in all, Chan Chan was a beautiful and populous city, which was well organized and a very fitting centre for a great empire.

The weaving of the Chimú women was fine, exactly planned like the compound walls and arranged in a sequence of steps. The range of colours available was considerable. All were permanent dyes, since they have survived in near original brilliance after nearly a thousand years in graves. The quantity of textiles made makes one think that the older system of workshops for groups of weavers was continued. But every woman had her own workbox of shuttles and spindles wound with coloured threads of cotton or alpaca wool. Usually she had a bundle of raw cotton ready for picking out and spinning into thread. Her needles were made of bronze and pierced with eyes in modern style. Normally she would be accompanied in the grave with a simple back-strap loom with a couple of heddles. Often it was occupied by an unfinished piece of tapestry, perhaps the last work of her hands. The dead lady usually wore a long cotton tunic and sandals, a broad band of colourful tapestry around her waist and often a shawl. Her hair was covered with embroidered net. Earrings, necklace and wristlets were worn, often, in the better class graves, made of gold and inlaid with turquoise or copper carbonate and shell.

The men wore a short tunic and loincloth, with a head-dress often made of coiled slings. They also wore decorative belts and much personal jewellery. The greater warriors had shirts entirely covered with pictures made of coloured feathers, and they also wore a fine feather head-dress. Their huge ear ornaments were of wood, gold plated and inlaid. They were often buried with arms, instead of the workboxes of their womenfolk. The Chimú noblemen must have presented a splendid sight in their colourful clothes with masses of gold and silver ornaments on their persons. This, all set out against their painted city, must have made a spectacle of brilliance hard to find in any other part of the world.

For processions and dances they had plenty of music. From

Chimu carved wooden work box, 15th century A D.

their Mochica predecessors they had inherited shell trumpets and coiled ceramic horns as well as panpipes of cane and pottery. They added wooden gongs and bronze bell-shaped percussion instruments. Rattles of bone, and bronze chain jangles mounted on palm wood rods, made a rhythmic accompaniment. They carried small circular drums, beaten with a stick which carried the rhythms of their singing. We know nothing of their music, but it must have been strongly rhythmic and loud enough to overcome the beating of the tambourines, gongs and rattles, and the tunes of the trumpets. Strangely enough, they seem to have had no stringed instruments. A musicologist, Mr William Yeomans, on a visit to the British Museum demonstrated that a pottery conch shell could be made to play a tune by putting the hand at various depths into the central coil of the 'shell'. So it is probable that such horns could be employed in making a melodic line. The one he used was Mochica in origin, but similar instruments were made by the Chimú people. The nature of the scale used by the Peruvians is not clear: it has been suggested that it was pentatonic, but also there is a strong suggestion that a twelve-tone scale was used. However, we have no record. The Spaniards, when they heard Peruvian music, commented upon the quality of its sadness, but we must remember that sixteenth-century people had views on music which differ from our own. But that there was plenty of music, and that it was rhythmic and noisy is not in dispute.

The Chimú fishermen continued to make small boats of bundled reeds, from which they angled with bronze fishhooks. They also used hand nets, and sometimes two reed canoes would encircle a shoal of fish with a seine net. The pottery shows innumerable scenes of fishing, which is only natural. It was the main source of food, and some of the fish are shown in the guise of powerful spirit beings. The Chimú also used the sailing balsa raft for coastal trade. The raft had a cabin amidships in which goods could be kept above the reach of the waves. There was a steersman who worked a series of centre-boards for directing the raft across the wind, and a triangular sheer-legs type of mast which supported a big sail. Such vessels were propelled by a number of paddlers who drove the boat forward by rhythmic strokes of their broad-bladed paddles. A few of the rafts had steering paddles as well as the centre boards. They were very navigable and used for coastal trade, though Thor Heyerdahl's adventure showed that they could also be navigated a thousand miles out to sea. The arts of the navigator seem to have been well known to the Chimú, since in their later days it was on a Chimú balsa that a future Supreme Inca ventured out as far as the Pacific atolls.

Trade inland was taken from town to town on the backs of llama trains or human porters. The slow llama could carry at most forty pounds, but the porter was capable of trotting with a load which might weigh more than a hundred pounds, held up by a tump line round his forehead. The choice depended on the nature of the journey. Messengers, of course, travelled light and ran from one staging post to another on the roads. The coastal trails across the sands were beaten down and marked by rows of tree stumps on either side of the route. The local inhabitants had the duty of clearing the paths after each sandstorm. They were able to trace the route by the rows of tree stumps. Alongside the sandy coastal roads, the unproductive sands provided cosy nests for the burial of the dead, whose remains stretch for miles, where they have been dug up by grave robbers. But in ancient times these places were kept sacred, and nothing was disturbed. The amount of gold buried with the dead makes it quite clear that the resting places were not disturbed even to assuage the Inca conqueror's thirst for the 'Tears of the Sun'. Meanwhile, the messengers trotted by carrying their messages neatly knotted up on coloured strings, for these *quipús* were as common among the coastal peoples as among the Inca.

Towns were built on sandy or rocky land near the river valleys. Some irrigation canals were dug on either side of the rivers in Mochica times. But the great increase in population during the Chimú period of rule made further diversion of water coming from the mountains in the short and violent rivers, imperative. New channels at differing levels were opened up, and considerable areas of alluvial earth were watered and proved richly productive. There was a little terracing of the lower slopes of hills, but nothing when compared to the great areas of terracing which were common in the highland regions. The Chimú area of rule was thenceforward well fed, with beans, squash and maize, to which other local food plants were added, including the peppers and the ground nut which was cultivated as richly as the highlanders cultivated the potato. The coastlands also produced the large tubers of the sweet potato. Constant hunting had reduced the supplies of venison, but the flesh of sea lions, as well as an inexhaustible supply of fish, provided a very good living for the population. This was indeed a rich civilization.

It appears that the Gran Chimú was an autocratic ruler aided by a council of officials in his service. The religious side of life was controlled by a group of carefully graded priests who conducted the ceremonies of the gods for the benefit of the state. There were nobles apparently of hereditary rank and a great mass of citizens, who included traders who commanded balsa rafts and caravans of

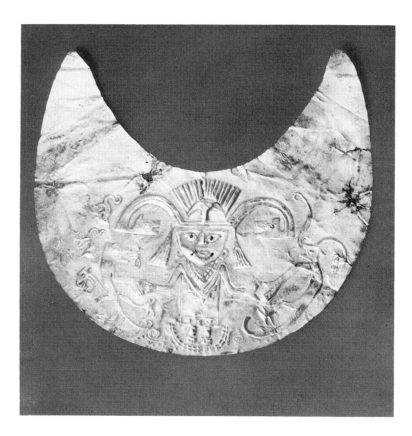

Chimu silver pendant with figure of deity, 15th century AD.

llamas. They traded up and down the coasts, going north with the currents of the ocean and south before the winds. Just what were their rewards is not apparent. Similarly we do not know how the people working in handicraft production workshops were rewarded. It may be that they were drafted to work for the state, or it may be that they retained a proportion of their products; but of anything resembling money as a medium of exchange there is no trace.

The amount of production from the organized workshops must have been phenomenal. Though when we consider that a woman's gown would take up some thirty kilometres of thread, the quantity of labour is not so excessive. It is not clear whether the produce of the workshops belonged to the supreme authority or to the district chiefs, for distribution or exchange. There must have been some organized form of exchange of manufactured produce, and probably the *quipu* records were important means of calculating the amounts produced of any commodity. It is probable that there was some centralized control somewhat like that imposed by the Inca.

In the production of pottery there was also some attempt at

Chimu clay relief from the 'Huaca del dragón' near Chan-Chan, 13th century AD.

mass production, since many of the vessels were made from moulded sheets of clay luted together, so that many designs are repeated in collections of ceramics of this culture. Most pottery was of a grey reduced fired ware, often burnished but sometimes with black burnished areas distinguished from the dark grey matt background. Many of the matt surfaced pots, when filled with water, show a silvery surface tone as if they were made to imitate the silver vessels of the upper-class households. Vessels in silver and gold are similar in form to the ceramics; in fact, the designs of the ceramic vessels are more suited to metal work than pottery. While the majority of Chimú vessels were of black ware, a proportion is also made in red ware prepared by the usual open firing with a good supply of oxygen. The designs of the red-ware pots are exactly the same as the black, and many are known in which the same set of moulds has been used to make pots in both red and black firings. In the north there is a number of pottery vessels, also imitating metal forms, which are washed over in a cream slip and decorated with red painted lines and scrolls. They may represent a late hang-over of Mochica art. In all regions of the Chimú kingdom the loop spouts of vases continued, but the loop was flat sided and decorated by a moulded row of small birds or animals. The idea of a restricted pouring area was continued, but the technique of making it had become a metal-workers' convention used by potters.

The metallurgists and jewellers had a field day under the Chimú rulers. Gold, copper and silver were placer-mined or sometimes dug out of the walls of cliffs beside the rivers. It seems that the Chimú had a highly developed metal technology, and no doubt they included in their numbers some highly skilled technicians, for there had always been a local tradition of metal work. Their equipment was very simple. Smelting was done in pottery crucibles placed in clay vessels filled with charcoal. They had no bellows, but the draught was supplied by a number of men sitting round the vessel and blowing the charcoal fire through bronze tubes. Of course, only a pound or two of metal could be treated at one time. Gold and silver in the crucibles were mixed with small amounts of copper to give them greater strength. Some of the metallurgists mixed copper with tin and sometimes black manganese ore. This produced a bronze, though without any exact device for weighing amounts the composition of the bronze was extremely variable. It is strange that in the central coast of Peru an invention was made of balanced scales for weighing small amounts of precious stones. But this brilliant invention was very local, probably the work of the jewellers of the small state of Cuismancu.

Ingots of metal were hammered out into sheets of very even thinness. These were hammered over reliefs set on blocks of smooth stone, producing *repoussé* ornament. The edges of the design were made into raised ridges by pressure on the under side by a bone tool. Then the raised lines were polished by stone rasps until they parted and the full design of the ornament fell loose from the sheet. Many ornaments were fitted with little pendants held in place by thin strips of metal or by loops of wire welded onto the surfaces. Considering the primitive nature of their tools, the standard of workmanship is remarkably high. The vessels of silver and gold for use in the palaces of the nobles reproduce the general forms of pottery but in a metallurgical tradition. The narrow spouted vases are made in several sections welded

together, and the open work bridges between the double spouts are often of intricate mythological designs. There are many golden vessels in collections, but the amounts of silver far outnumber them. Sometimes the silver has a great deal of copper alloyed with it so that excavated vessels look quite green. However, there are also some vessels made in nearly pure copper, a difficult metal to work and a mute testimony to Chimú skills.

The bronzes were used for musical instruments, tubular trumpets, cymbals and chain jangles with small cascabels attached. There was also a kind of large tweezer which was possibly a rhythmic instrument. But tools included tweezers for depilation, knives with elaborately decorated handles and curved blades, spear head and two-piece helmets joined across sides and top. Great masks were made of gold, silver or bronze to go on top of mummy bundles. Then personal ornaments included *repoussé* wristlets and anklets several inches in depth, chains and pendants, some nose pendants and many great earrings of wood cased in *repoussé* gold. There are fantastic head ornaments of which the main decorations are flexible and must have vibrated when the wearer danced. Also the Chimú delighted in tunics to

Chimu base silver vessel in the form of a dog with two puppies, 13th or 14th century AD.

Chimu gourd bowl with mythological figures inlaid in coloured shell and jade, 12th or 13th century AD.

which little plaques in the form of metal animals and birds were sewn. All in all their civilization had a gorgeous golden aspect.

The dead were cared for. In many cases the viscera were removed and the cavities washed out with some preservative fluid. Otherwise the body was simply sun dried, and then it was dressed and trussed up with the head resting on the knees and the hands folded over the shins. Then the whole bundle was made up with spare garments and sheets of textile. It became a big conical bundle to which was attached a false head, sometimes of textile, and sometimes of painted wood. Around the body the tools of daily life were packed, and the whole was usually deposited in a mat lined grave. The care taken with these burials shows that the people had an expectation of a future life. Though the pots sometimes show a dried body, there is no real evidence that the bodies of the dead were ever brought out in ceremonial processions as was the case with the Incas.

Perhaps the grim conditions and the thin air of the high *altiplano* influenced the Inca outlook on life and helped them to develop their rather grim puritanism. Many of their towns and villages were more than two miles above sea level. Of course the

Inca were an extended family, not a nationality. They were kept separate in many ways from the mass of the population, but by the time of the last Inca, the twelfth, their numbers were many thousands, out of a population of some seven million in the empire.

The Inca kingdom in Cuzco did not increase for more than a century. The danger point came when the Inca family took over the whole town. There was a movement among the other mountain tribes to destroy the rulers before their pretensions made them all powerful. The current chief, named Yahuar Huaccac, was pusillanimous. He temporized and held some conferences with those who would destroy the Incas. Eventually a family council deprived the old man of his powers. They chose a younger man, properly born from the previous Sapa Inca and his sister, to govern them. He took the name of Inca Viracocha, greatly daring to name himself after the creator. In a series of sudden unexpected attacks from the rear of the enemy, he eventually defeated the Chanca and their allies. His generalship seemed inspired, and suddenly the Inca family found themselves masters of all the Peruvian Andean region, extending as far south as ancient Tiahuanaco. The Incas had arrived as the dominant power in Peru.

The most important progress, however, was in the reign of the ninth Inca, Pachacuti Yupanqui Inca. He was a great organizer and is credited with a reorganization of the army and a stricter social grading of the nation and its conquered territories. He rebuilt Cuzco as a sacred centre for an empire which he felt to be Tahuantinsuyu, the Four Quarters (of the world). Here were the two great ceremonial squares, palaces and administrative building. The strings knotted up with records of the empire were kept in an annexe to his palace. There was also the Temple of the Sun with its formal garden of images of food plants, especially made of gold and silver. All around the temple was a massive cornice of gold, and inside a golden wall stretched right across the building decorated in *repoussé* work with symbols of the creation, the sun and moon and the first Incas. The place for the creator was just a blank area near the symbol of the Southern Cross. It was the apparently empty 'Coal Sack' in the Milky Way. The Inca believed that Con Tiki Viracocha was formless and invisible in his home above.

While Pachacuti Yupanqui organized the empire and worked from Cuzco, his son and heir Topa Inca led the army on further campaigns. Most importantly he led a great army northwards along the mountain roads towards Quito. He reached his objective and so damaged the power of that kingdom that the people of

Carved wooden figure of seated man with phallic headdress, from Peru, 15th century AD.

Chimu golden pendant with repoussé mask, from Peru, 13th or 14th century AD.

Quito never again were a threat to the Incas. Then unexpectedly he turned the main body of his army to the coast and marched southwards. Minor attacks were made to the south of the Chimú kingdom, probably to draw their army away from the great coastal cities. The main force swept irresistibly over the lands of the Chimú. The whole of the Chimú culture was subverted. But then the king of the land and great numbers of skilled workmen were taken as captives to Cuzco. There they found themselves honoured. The wise Pachacuti knew well that the Chimu had many skills which the Inca wanted. So the captives were used as teachers of systems of recording, of metal work and of textile weaving. But not of pottery or of religion.

The great temples of the Chimú were left with their own gods who were worshipped by the people, but each temple had attached to it by the Inca's command a special building devoted to the worship of Inti, the Inca sun god. He was appointed by his children to be God of Gods, ruler of all. He claimed all the gold in the land for the Inca, and also a tribute was laid on the Chimú people, paid in woodwork, weaving and food stuffs. Coloured cotton yarn was also contributed. The Chimú recording by *quipus* was somewhat richer than that of the Incas, so the new rulers adopted it. The difference was that all records were sent to Cuzco so that the Inca, as child of the sun, would have all control in his hands. The province was ruled by its own prince, but he had been married to a young lady of pure Inca blood. Thus the rule of the sun's family would be assured, and the prince was educated in Inca ways in the palace of his father-in-law.

After the conquest of the Chimú Topa Inca led his armies to take over the many small kingdoms and cities which had developed over the southern half of the coast where the Nasca culture had once flourished. The conquest was easy, especially as many of the tribes asked to become part of the Inca empire, to share in its work and the benefits stemming from Inca organization. There was intense pressure built up by Inca envoys in these states to induce them to participate. Those who could be frightened heard of a chief who was captured, killed and dried with a wooden frame inside his emptied abdomen which was used as a drum. Nobody wished for such a scornful ending. So they considered it best to lead their people into the Inca state where nobody died of hunger, where even the ravages of earthquake and storm were repaired at speed. The more intelligent chiefs thought similarly of the reality of the material benefits to be gained by Inca rule. One can have little doubt that the diplomatic offensive was masterminded by the Supreme Inca Pachacuti.

Eventually the time came, in 1471, for Pachacuti, now grown old, to return to the sun. The powerful Topa Inca succeeded him on the throne. There were great ceremonies for the burial of Pachacuti, more solemn than those with which any of his predecessors had been honoured. But the end was the same. The rocky mass of his palace was fully furnished, and his servants cared for it. Here on a throne were seated the dried bodies of Pachacuti and his wife Mama Anarauque. Once a year the bodies were seated on gold-covered biers and taken to sit in the great sun temple, along with their ancestors. There was sorrow in the hearts of the people, and the keepers of history brought out the painted boards which told the story of the great reign. There seems to have been some idea that the sun might one day send them back to live on earth.

But now Topa Inca was installed. His workmen built him a new

The Sacsahuaman fortress above Cuzco, Inca family work, 14th or 15th century AD.

Golden figure of girl from Lambayeque, Peru, 15th or 16th century AD.

palace of grey granite. It was massive and low with high thatched roofs of golden grass. Inside its simple rooms, there were treasures accumulated from his wars. There was a great hall for meetings and other halls for the sons of chiefs from foreign lands who would be married to Inca girls and indoctrinated into Inca ways of thought. The new Emperor had to pass his vigil in the sun temple, in the presence of his ancestors sitting silently in the niches. Later the High Priest would crown him with the sacred *llautu*. This was a band of several coils of the deep red wool from the wild guanaco, dyed with a special dye kept for this textile and Inca garments. Then in it was placed a wooden pin which supported a little square banner as big as the palm of one's hand. It was edged with a pendant fringe also of red. At the top were two blue and yellow feathers from a sacred mountain bird. They were the true symbol of the Inca in all his lonely glory as the true divine ruler of Tahuantinsuyu.

As at the annual festival of the return of the sun, there was a great deal of dancing, from the circle of nobles holding a rope of golden wires as they danced in a ring, down to the linear dances of the common people in which men and women faced each other singing and dancing. The music was mainly of drums and flutes, beautiful and in a minor key. As the occasion came to a close, the new Inca gave a donation of *chicha* (a fermented drink made from maize chewed by maidens), and the population of Cuzco became drunk and fell asleep against any convenient wall. They were happy that the new ruler had obeyed all the rules and so would have a happy reign among them. But though they loved him, they might never look on his face. Whenever he passed by, the people bowed to the ground and covered their eyes lest his glory blind them. Was he not the representative of the sun on earth?

Topa Inca was soon leading his armies. When battling along the edge of the Amazonian forests, he was informed that the Colla and their allies in the south of the mountains were in revolt. He turned his forces against them, slew many, took prisoners for execution and consolidated the position. Then, returning to Cuzco, he heard of a more distant event. The Calchaqui-Diaguita of northern Argentina had crossed the mountain passes far to the south and reached the Pacific coasts. No doubt he felt that this was a threat to the great concept of Tahuantinsuyu. To this he brought a cool mind and planned a campaign which would mean a march of some seven hundred miles along the mountains. He organized the army into groups from each region, but before them went a column of sappers. They levelled the trackways and hammered holes in cliffs to support beams carrying a roadway. They made the swinging suspension bridges over ravines and cleared the way steadily to enable the army to march. Meanwhile, hundreds of big balsa rafts took supplies of extra weapons and food along the coasts. They established depots to supply the army and, when they came near the coasts occupied by the Calchaqui, they awaited the approach of the armies. When this took place, the Inca forces, elated by their marvellous march and strengthened by the supplies of food and extra clothing from the fleet, attacked. The battle was fierce, but the enemy was decisively routed.

Topa Inca decreed that, for the time being, the southern boundary should be the River Maule, in what is now Chile. The roads constructed for the advance were consolidated and all this southern region was brought under Inca administration.

During the highland march the nobles were accompanied by their families. When a little Princess of some importance died, her body was dried, dressed and wrapped in layers of cloth. They were sad for the little girl and buried her in a corner of a cave with her favourite doll, a little silver figure dressed in woollen gown and red Inca cape held in place with a big silver pin. On the head was a pretty crown of feathers. The body of the Princess was found in 1961, a sad echo of the great march made by the armies of Topa Inca. But it is to be noted that the Indians of Peru lived only for the glory of their beneficent Inca, and every social group was ready to accept its fate as divinely led. Death was an incident of some importance but not of great terror.

After the conquest Topa Inca spent the remaining years of his reign consolidating the huge empire. His home life is said to have been extremely happy with his wife who was a little dwarf princess. She was a brilliant ruler of the powers of the moon, which was her official function, and had many kindly acts recorded of her. She was regarded as saner than her mother who had insisted that all her servants should be stark naked – but probably that lady had simply loved beauty. Topa Inca came to death in 1493. He had no knowledge that far to the north Christopher Columbus had found the way for Iron Age Europeans to reach America and return.

The next Supreme Inca was Huayna Ccapac, a wise man, who had earlier ventured with a fleet of rafts into the Pacific. After half a year he had returned with some strange brown skinned people with wavy hair. It is probable that he had discovered the Tuamotus. While Supreme Ruler, he expanded the realm of Tahuantinsuyu to the north. He came into conflict with the Cara rulers of Ecuador. There were fierce battles, and the Inca armies found these people almost their equals. However, Quito was finally captured. Huayna Ccapac was, of course, married to his sister when he took the throne. She was a great beauty with long

Golden beaker with repoussé decoration, typically Inca, early 16th century AD.

wavy hair who had always many servants around her. But even though she had borne him a son to succeed him, the Inca, used to many subsidiary wives, was smitten fatefully by love. His heart went out to a princess of Quito. He often established his Court in the northern city and made much of its inhabitants. It is little wonder that he deeply loved the sharp little boy whom the beloved princess bore him. Therein lay the fate of nations. The child was named Atahuallpa. His legitimately full-blooded Inca brother was Prince Huascar.

What influenced the mind of Huayna Ccapac is not certain. He was a great poet, a good administrator and a skilled commander. Did he think that Tahuantinsuyu must be abandoned for a smaller concept of an easily administered state? Or was his Inca way of thought clouded by a romantic illusion? He had but little knowledge of the coming threat from the north, where the Spaniards had settled Panama and were already planning to seek out a mysterious golden land to the south. He had no intimation of the destruction of Mexico. It is possible that the trading Indians who told Pizarro of the golden lands to the south might also have told the Peruvians of the strange men clad in grey iron who had appeared. But what capped everything was the appearance of strange, bearded men on the outskirts of the northern coasts. This was Pizarro's first ill-fated expedition. What were they? But almost as soon as the news reached him, Huayna Ccapac was taken ill with a pestilence. Was it one of the new diseases, such as smallpox, which the Spaniards had introduced to America? Whatever was afoot, Huayna Ccapac seems to have willed the division of Tahuantinsuyu. Quito and northern parts of Peru were to be ruled by Atahuallpa, and the southern regions were to remain with his son, the divine Inca Huascar.

It happened that Huascar was of a peaceable disposition. He moved back to Cuzco and was properly crowned there with the *borla* fringe. But Atahuallpa was aggressive. He had no real understanding of the divinity of the Supreme Inca. It seems that he held the view that the ruler was the man with the most efficient army. In this he had a great advantage because under his command were two Quitan generals, Quiz-quiz and Callcu chima. They organized a war on Cuzco. Huascar had an army equally large, but the Quitans arranged a two-pronged attack which progressively drove Huascar southwards. There were some four or five years of this campaign. The country was disorganized to a great extent, since the centre where tribute should have been sent for redistribution was no longer there. Eventually the legitimate Supreme Inca was captured. He was tied with ropes and led to captivity in a fortress some twenty miles outside of Cuzco.

Atahuallpa made himself Inca. Death would have been the reward of the priests if they had refused to invest him with the symbols of power. They compromised and allowed him his impious way. The country was paralysed.

It was shortly after the sad end of the civil war that the final landing of the Spaniards occurred. For more than half a year Pizarro's forces occupied the coast, controlled the passive population and consolidated their new territory. Probably the people had fatalistically identified the strangers with armour and horses as heavenly messengers sent to punish the country for the usurpation by Atahuallpa. There was practically no resistance. Then Pizarro heard that the false Inca was ready to meet him. In extreme danger before the immense Peruvian-Quitan armies, he evolved a daring plan. The false Inca was seized amid the slaughtered corpses of his bodyguard. But the Inca line was rendered impotent for the time, because Atahuallpa, hearing of the Spanish invasion, had ordered that Inca Huascar should be strangled in prison. After that there was a half century of confusion and struggle in which the Spaniards slew each other, and the legitimate Inca line was driven to submission or death. This series of petty campaigns brought to an end a great and enlightened civilization. Latin America still suffers from the loss.

In the century between the accession of Pachacuti Inca in 1438 to the fall of Atahuallpa in 1532, the Incas had made a tremendous change in Peruvian culture. For one thing they had unified the country under a benevolent dictatorship, and for another they had adapted and extended local customs particularly from the Chimú people, until the whole land was held together by a network of communications. They had built a social security system through which nobody could die from want and developed a national service of workers to repair houses and roads throughout the land. True, the population were mostly totally dependent on the bureaucracy headed by the Supreme Inca, but then they mostly accepted a loss of freedom as a good exchange for the conditions of plenty and security which marked the Inca regime. Peru has not enjoyed such a social welfare system since the early sixteenth century.

The Inca regime contributed nothing new to the material culture of Peru. Woven cloth was still made from hand spun wool on a simple back-strap loom. Pottery was made in local techniques, but more and more the Inca imposed a group of standard pottery forms and techniques. These involved a reversion to coiling as a method of building, but the quality of forms and beauty of surface were superb. Decoration was very simple, of geometric forms with an occasional fern leaf or a flower design.

Chimu silver beaker with face in relief, beaten out of a single block of metal, 14th or 15th century AD.

The infiltration of this ceramic style was irregular. In the Chimú kingdom it was adapted to a black ware technique as well as being often decorated rather more freely. In Ecuador it was taken over but in a coarser form, and occasionally it was made into figure vases, mostly representing a woman with a large vase on her back. But there are examples everywhere of some eight or nine standard vase forms, in approximately standard sizes.

The most ubiquitous of Inca pottery forms was the so-called *aryballus*. This was a pot with a shallow conical base and high domed body leading to a long narrow neck with a flaring lip. It had two strap handles at the sides of the body and a projecting nub, often in the form of an animal head on the upper part of the body. This was a device for keeping the pot upright when carried on the back. The tump line which went around the forehead of the woman carrying the load was threaded through the handles and brought up over the nub. Thus the upward pressure on the handles was balanced by a downward pull on the back of the vase. This form of vessel was made in several sizes, from a nine-inch-high model holding a pint up to huge vessels holding nine or ten gallons of liquid. Spilling was prevented by putting a skin cap over the flaring lip and tying it in position, often by a thread secured by passing through two small perforated lugs on the underside of the lip. Usually these vessels were decorated by vertical bands of geometric ornament over the fuller part of the body. They were used for carrying water, and at festival times they were filled with *chicha* or maize beer.

Cooking was done in a bowl very much like a casserole without a lid. The sides sloped a little inward, and it was carried by means

Two small Inca ceramic ladles, 16th century AD. Note the geometric decoration.

of two broad strap handles. Usually these vessels were decorated with a cream slip and a few narrow panels of geometric ornament. The food was ladled out and eaten from shallow dishes of various sizes, which usually had a stem handle ending in an animal head. The drinking cups were stemmed bowls with flared feet and usually a strap handle on one side near the rim. All this Inca pottery is marked by its perfection of form, balanced decoration and beautiful surface. Its presence at a site is definite proof of Inca influence, and the local variations only serve to emphasize the relative lateness of the Inca conquests.

Inca woodwork was carved with bronze and polished with soft stone and sand. It is massive and simple in form. There were carvings of jaguars and llamas, bowls and drinking apparatus in which the *chicha* was poured into a bowl from which it ran through carved runnels into a spout, whence it poured directly into the mouth of the drinker. The major wooden product was a large goblet with flaring sides and often an animal head on the rim. This was the *kero*, used not only for social drinking but on all great occasions for pouring out a libation to the gods. Thus it was usually made of wood of considerable thickness, often in excess of a centimetre. The sides were engraved with geometric designs, and sometimes shallow hollows were prepared to be filled with coloured mastic. This last form of decoration became much more popular after the Spanish conquest. We hear of low benches made to serve as seats and thrones, which were elaborately decorated, and for the Inca they were ornamented with gold. But none of them has survived. Similarly the lacquered boards which held a pictorial history of the Incas are not available to us. The conquerors destroyed all the history of their victims, and the boards were burned on a bonfire in Cuzco.

Metalwork was mainly influenced by the Inca family's total monopoly of gold. Hence all gold work of the period was the work of the Inca family and its craftsmen. The large ring earrings with *repoussé* ornament were worn by the nobles whom the Spaniards later dubbed 'Big Ears'. The spoons, ornamented *kero* vessels and the great works of decoration in Coricancha, the House of Gold where the sun god lived in several images of which the smallest was the holiest, were all Inca works by privileged noble artisans. It was in vast quantities, and apart from family treasures the great mass of the precious metal was either mined or conquered from the palaces and persons of the Chimú. The Incas did not disturb the graves of the dead, and so the buried treasures remained quietly with their original owners. Silver was much used, and, although it has often deteriorated into a black oxide, a great deal has remained in the very dry climate of the coastal deserts. Vases

Ceramic *paccha* used for pouring *chicha* (maize beer) into the mouths of noblemen, typically Inca, early 16th century AD. The drink was poured into the upper vessel and ran past the ear of maize into the spout, which takes the form of a digging stick end.

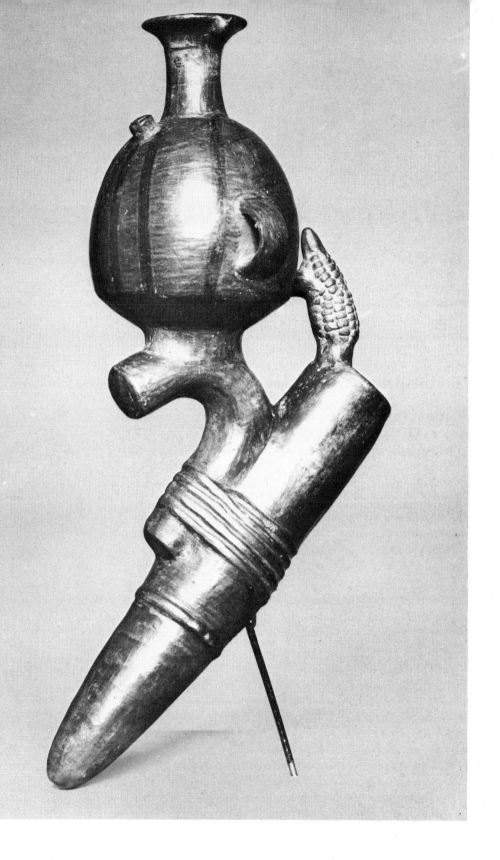

and pendants were the principal products, though many figures of hollow cast work are known. These are of naked men and women, all smooth and without waists but with natural sex organs. The Incas were quite simple in those matters. Fact and clarity were right, and so, while having very prudish regulations about social conduct, they were never prurient.

The other important branch of metalwork was the use of bronze. This was made up into decorative moon-shaped knives with an upright handle from the centre of the blade; chisels, often with a hollow rattle on the grip, and all manner of knives and hoe blades. There was also a very typical Inca line in the six- or eight-pointed stars which formed the heads of fighting clubs. Analysis presents a picture of a wild admixture of alloys in varying degrees. Ann Kendall has pointed out that it seems probable that the mixture bore a relationship to the work it was expected to do. This is probably true, but as scales were not in use for anything heavier than an ounce, it is probable that the metal workers had worked out their mixtures by the handful or finger pinch of material. Hence to our critical analysis the variation in mixture must seem random. Of course the metal workers were a special class in the population and were concentrated near the mines whence they obtained their raw material. They were the equivalent of a trade guild, and they paid their tribute to the Inca in the form of finished work for either the military or religious storehouses. They received allowances of food and clothing from the public store rooms on a fixed scale recorded on the *quipus*.

The miners were conscript labour, doing this service in payment of their taxes. They worked a shift system, and the draft of men was required to work for only about three or four months at a time. The method was to sink an adit or sometimes a shaft from which adits radiated. The mining was not far underground, and it was rare for a mine tunnel, even in rich ore-bearing ground, to go for more than eighty yards into the rocks. They worked by torchlight in these deeper mines. The spoil was spread on a sheet of cloth and then bundled up and brought to the overseer at the mouth. The system was slow but quite efficient, and the miners were not overworked. Often the ores were taken in packs of fifty pounds on the backs of llamas to spurs of the mountains where there were larger furnaces. The ore was loaded into crucibles in big pottery bowls full of charcoal. When the fire was lit, the holes made in the pottery furnaces permitted the mountain winds to blow through and make a draught which increased the temperatures. The mixture of copper ores and tin ore or zinc ore was made in the furnace, so that the resultant bronze would be safer than if they had tried to melt out the highly oxidizable copper by itself.

From a modern point of view production was not high; but it was quite sufficient to cover a regular demand for tools and weapons made from the most usable alloy.

Bronze entered into women's life a good deal. They used knives for cutting up food, and bronze spindles and needles. There was also a cosmetic use for the numbers of various sized depilatory tweezers, and the use of the knife for trimming hair on blocks of wood. Such knives also cut the cloth from their looms when a length was completed.

The women of Peru were always good weavers. The Inca made little change, except for their own use. Complex chequer patterns became popular. Little girls learned how to pick cotton or collect llama wool as soon as they could toddle. By the time they were six they had begun a lifetime's work spinning thread on a little hand spindle with a whorl at one end. Everywhere a woman walked, she kept her spindle busily twisting thread. A simple shirt would take a mile of thread. Then, by the time a girl was eight or nine, she would be sufficiently advanced to work a simple loom and learn the arts of tapestry, *kelim* and other techniques. She had also learned the use of dyes and their preparation. The result of all this work was that no one went ill-dressed in Inca Peru. The production of cloth was phenomenal, and vast quantities of cloth paid in tribute filled the Inca storehouses and gave relief in times of disaster. Even the army storehouses were kept full of quilted war shirts and wraps. Cotton was grown in three natural colours, white, pale green and pale brown. But there were many vegetable and mineral dyes. Llama wool was not much used because it was coarse, but the vicuña produced much more delicate wool, combed from its skin, though this was reserved for the Sun Maidens who wove it for the Incas. Alpaca wool was the variety most used for clothing.

The ordinary Peruvian family was an assisted self-supporting unit. Father dug the ground, and mother planted the seed. Father built the house and kept his part of the irrigated terraces in good repair. He also built and repaired the house as necessary. Mother cooked and made the clothing. Little boys scared the birds off the crops and caught small animals. Mother looked after the guinea pigs which were kept as food supplies. The girls were always busy spinning or weaving, helping with the fields and the cleaning. Under the Incas the making of terraces to hold up the soil on sloping ground was greatly extended, and water runways were built. So every family had its share of land and water. Of the food grown and textiles woven, approximately two-thirds were paid in taxes, half to the sun priests and half to the Inca. The remainder of the materials kept the family reasonably well.

The terraced slopes of the Inca Intihuatana Hill at Machupicchu, Peru, 14th or 15th century AD.

Nobody could slack in Peru, since every family in each little settlement was responsible to its neighbours. Maybe a woman was untidy, and then she was snubbed by the others; but on the whole the village kept a balance of productiveness partly as a result of natural emulation. They were never lost, since one householder in ten had to keep records of the production of each family, and one in fifty kept the records of the whole village. If there was a great storm or an earthquake, a messenger went to the nearest town, and the local governor would summon help. A special repair corps of the army would rebuild houses. The storehouses of the Inca were opened, and food and new clothing were supplied. It was then all recorded in knots on the *quipus*, and the incident closed.

All boys had a period of army service, roughly between the ages of fifteen and twenty. They had already been sent at twelve to be initiated as men and go through various strenuous games and exercises. So they were quite prepared for the trotting march of the armies and the hardships of long journeys and sleeping rough. The army was fed and clothed, and its discipline was strict but good. They soon realized that they must all work together equally if they were to remain friendly and happy with one another. There were several grades of command, but the highest ranks and continuous service were reserved for members of the Inca family. Some of the conscripts were sent to the labour corps for repairing houses and bridges, and some of the ordinary soldiers stayed in the army. A very few of these might win high honour for bravery and initiative, and still fewer might be selected to be honoured by the Inca. They might become local *curacas*, district chiefs, and even be allowed to marry a princess of Inca blood, thus making sure that their children would enter the nobility. But for most young men their army service was a chance to see Tahuantinsuyu, to work for their Sapa Inca and then to return to their village. Then they would be encouraged to marry. The girls of the right age would be available, or at least a few would. Questions of relationship restricted the choice, and of course the approval of the officials must be obtained. Then at an annual festival all the pairs of young people from the village would go to the town, and there would be a marriage. The *quipucamoyoc* would tie his knots and enter them on the list of families as householders. On their return there would be a small house provided by their neighbours, and land and water made available. For a year they were tax free, or for the first year or two of each baby born to them. But for the rest of their lives they would continue with household work in the village, enjoying the passage of the seasons and the friendship of their neighbours.

They paid taxes regularly, and when they became old, their liability was reduced, and they were allotted communal help, food and clothing from the royal storehouses. When they died, they were sun-dried and the bodies hidden in a burial cave after a farewell service.

To this regular routine of the Inca state there were many exceptions. When children were eight or nine years old, the government inspectors from the town would come to examine them. If certain boys were intellectually alert, and certain girls were beautiful and expert at weaving, they were taken away from their families to go to training schools, and there the boys became simple administrators, perhaps rising to become skilled *quipuc-amayocs*. The girls were taken to a special temple and fine housing in the Cuzco itself. There they became the Virgins of the Sun and were taught the most wonderful kinds of weaving in vicuña wool and how to serve the temples. Most of them would be married off to nobles whom the Inca wished to honour, but always many remained weaving and working, until some decided to spend all their lives in the service of religion. There they tended the temples and taught successive generations of young women.

Every village had its simple teachers who taught the rudiments of social behaviour and good manners and the simple basis of *quipu* recording, so that at least they could knot up cords recording their activities to be given to the heads of the village when the time came.

Thus ordinary life went on. Women worked and chatted as they ground the maize or worked in the fields. Men went out to trap animals or repair walls as well as doing the hard digging with their copper-shod digging sticks with the footrest to give more power. It appears that they were a quiet people not given to disorder, and happily to be found dancing and drinking at the great festivals. In the Inca state at its best there was food for all, housing and clothing assured and a very small chance of advancement for brilliant children. But the Inca family, with their great golden earplugs, were masters of all, and of them the Supreme Inca was lord of all, under only the gods.

Of course human individuality asserted itself and sometimes led people into trouble with the regulations. For them there was law wisely administered by judges in the towns. They were Inca judges, but their position and even their lives were in jeopardy if they were biased in their judgments. Severe crimes were punished by death, often of a horrifying nature, such as being hung up and slit open so that the interior organs fell out in public. Less horrendous crimes sometimes merited mutilation; a hand or foot might be cut off, or a nose or ears. This would mark the

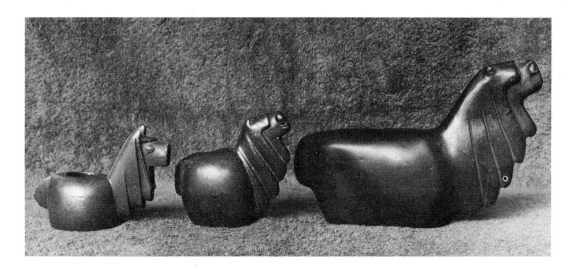

Three Inca stone vessels in the form of alpacas, used to magic the fields, 15th century AD.

offender so that others would not copy his crime. If the mutilations were severe, the victim was clothed and fed and forced to sit at the entrance of the nearest town as a warning to all comers. There was little imprisonment in Peru except for such notables as the unfortunate Inca Huascar. Deadly crimes were encouraging revolt, denigrating the Sapa Inca, insulting the gods and adultery. Theft and causing a minor affray were the causes of mutilation. But theft was very rare in a land where all shared in the national prosperity.

The priests conducted public worship, with each new moon and at special harvest and planting festivals. There were also two annual ceremonies for the sun god, his return to Peru and the time of his furthest journey, when a great penitential ceremony was held so that the new year should begin with a cleansing from sin and the renewal of the whole nation. At these times little trays were made and the sins of the people tied up in knots and pieces of old cloth. They were filled at a religious gathering, and as everyone wept for past misdeeds, the trays were taken to the nearest river and launched. It was hoped that if the trays drifted safely out of sight the sins of the past were forgiven, and the community entered the new year all fresh and clean. For the holy city of Cuzco the Inca conducted a special ceremony in which the sins of the community were tied on the back of a black llama, which was then sent to wander and die in the wilderness. Even the Supreme Inca as well as all his subjects covered his head with a white cloth and lamented his sins. These were sins against the creator rather than just against the sun. The depth of the festival, though temporarily governed by the sun's position, went out into the mysterious great darkness of creation.

The sun festival was one in which all the peoples of Peru rejoiced at the sun's turning towards them. The people of Cuzco allowed visitors to bring tribute from the four provinces of Tahuantinsuyu, but they were afterwards turned away from the holy place where Inca Roca had allowed the golden wedge to sink into the earth. So in Cuzco the local people came to rejoice. The Inca on that one vigil laid off his crown and prayed alone in Coricancha, the House of Gold, home of the sun. His dead ancestors all looked on. Then in the morning a ray of light burst in and struck the golden wall. The Inca arose and went out in his most splendid costume to conduct the rejoicings. Great dances were held in which the nobles performed a ring dance holding in their hands a chain which is said to have been made of gold. In the great square the Inca himself met a sacred pure white llama caparisoned in red. He talked to the llama and it answered back, so that he could interpret its words as a prophecy of coming luck for the year ahead. Then all shouted and sang. There were many processions and much drinking. Once the Peruvians sat down and refused to work because Inca Pachacuti wisely halved their beer ration, but he never repeated the experiment. After some days of dancing and drinking, the festival ended, the people fell asleep and next day outsiders were once more admitted to Cuzco.

Basically the Inca culture was designed for villages around ceremonial centres, of which the heart was the simple magnificence of Cuzco, the Navel of the World. The other towns were largely collecting and distribution centres where the whole of Inca life was planned for the welfare of the local people as well as for the glory of the sun and his child the Inca. The towns were also to some extent tribal capitals. The district was controlled from them, and all the people of the district wore forms of dress and ornament which marked them out from all others. This was important, since the Inca officials could see immediately if strangers were visiting the community and who they were. If there were too many gatherings with people from other districts, there were enquiries. Always vigilance was exerted to detect any kind of discontent. If possible, remedies were found. But there was always a fear that revolts might be planned, and so by the system they could be detected and stamped upon in time.

Sometimes revolts against the Inca did take place. Usually local mismanagement was to blame, but old tribal loyalties died hard. If the revolt was on a large scale, the people of the district were brought into town, and half of them from every area were sent away. This was a mild punishment because the migrants were sent to areas similar in nature to those they had left. They were also excused taxes for a year while they settled into their new homes.

Inca wooden *kero* with face painted with mastic and decorated panels, 16th century AD.

Thus a peaceful balance was assured, and suffering was kept to a minimum.

Among the Inca clan there were also signs of rank. This usually took the form of an ornament worn in the head-dress which recorded the rank and duties of its wearer. All men of the clan wore huge golden earrings, and they had the right to wear fine *cumpi* cloth with specific designs which also appear to have given some clue as to their position. They were the administrators of Tahuantinsuyu and must keep watch. Of course their organization was disrupted by the civil war when Atahuallpa seized power. It is probable that there was an increase of spying activities and local failures in record keeping. So the Spanish writers had a distorted picture of affairs.

The Inca clan had its origin in the multitude of wives who were allowed for each Inca, beside the sister who was his wife and queen. Great nobles were allowed only two or rarely three wives, but the Inca himself was obliged to marry notable young ladies from the subject peoples and also had the choice of the most beautiful girls from the *acclahuasi*, the House of the Sun Virgins. In that natural world, so different from the erotic fantasy of the Chimú, there were many babies born to the Supreme Inca. These were all members of a lineage named after their father. Thus by the time of the eleventh Inca there were eleven groups within the clan, and they were numbered by the thousand. They were in fact an aristocracy who, under the dictatorship of the current Sapa Inca, controlled the whole of the welfare state of Peru.

The Inca girls learned many aspects of weaving and wore pretty clothes, the long gown with a highly decorated waist band, and the cloak held in place by a great golden pin, or more often of silver, the moon metal. They wore sandals, bracelets and necklaces, and on their heads there was a folded piece of fine white cloth. This was just like the dress of all Peruvian women, but it was finer and more decorated. Apart from being housed in palaces, their lives were much like those of the ordinary women. The most powerful ones had servants, but all were expected to spin wool or cotton, and most had a working knowledge of pottery. Some of them gained a reputation for wisdom, but for most life was just a round of household duties and social gossip. Even where they had attendants to do the housework, there was little for a woman to do in that male dominated society. Yet they made much that was beautiful, and we can enjoy the perfection of their weaving and pottery today.

The men of the Inca clan were employed in a wide variety of administrative works. The provincial governors and civic chiefs were the highest grades, but the readers of *quipus* and keepers of

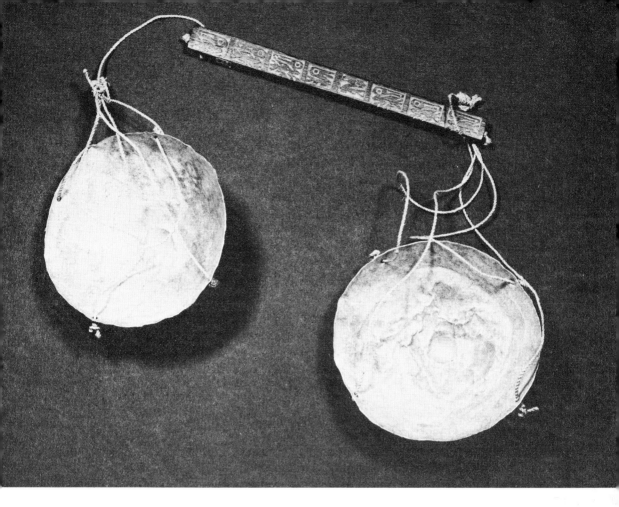

Jeweller's scales, wooden bar and metal trays, from Cuismancu, central Peruvian coast, 15th century AD.

records were important, and there were vast numbers of inspectors. They watched over and recorded the work on roads and bridges. They were important in the army, as commanders and also as organizers of the commissariat. They checked the tributes brought to the royal storehouses and arranged the constantly changing quotas of produce from each area of the land. In fact the whole organization of the country was in the hands of an hereditary civil service. The lower grades of the administration were not Inca by birth, however. They were the village chiefs, the commanders of labour groups and the heads of a hundred and of ten families. But when these took their reports to the cities, they made their statements to officials wearing the great golden earrings of the Children of the Sun.

When the Incas, in their earlier days, decided to build the great Hawks' Eyrie Fortress (Sacsahuaman) defending Cuzco, the menfolk became the masons, moving the enormous rocks with levers and rollers and battering them so that the flattened surfaces fitted precisely. It was an immense concept, with its three great terraces of re-entrant angles and the enormous circular tower in the centre. Entirely of Inca workmanship, it still shows us their determination to rule with power. Strangely it was never used by the Inca, but it served as a refuge for the Spaniards in the sixteenth century during an Inca-led revolt. Such a work for the cause of their clan power was a great cementation of the clan and set a tradition which all remembered with pride. Not until the revolt by Atahuallpa, who through his father was a member, did the clan find itself divided.

It is in the Chimú area that one notes the sad effect of the Inca conquest, since the fine goldwork disappears, and the style of the pottery degenerates, often trying to imitate Inca forms and becoming inadequate in its design. Such a failure of native art is a frequent result of conquest by foreigners. One sees it in Eastern art of the last century. In Peru the change would probably not have lasted long, but before the traditions could either assimilate or produce a developing hybrid art, the Spanish conquest brought native arts to a halt except for everyday utilitarian materials. Everywhere the change in social structure brought about a collapse of the old Inca organization. There was a real regression because all the teaching facilities and the social welfare programmes were abandoned. The substitution of European feudalism brought about a period of hunger and isolation, especially among the mountain peoples. Art became the servant of the Spaniards and rapidly copied and even excelled its models.

The Inca culture of Peru was the capstone to an arch of rising skill and centralization of governments. The real unification of many tribes and kingdoms into an organized empire was something no other American people had achieved. Its success was a reflection on the weakness of the divided cultures of earlier Peru. In fact, tribal division and a constant balance of warfare was the main retardation principal of the American Indian race. The Incas of Peru alone overcame it. We shall never know whether they would have extended the concept of Tahuantinsuyu to the whole of South America, but we must remember that the collapse came from within. The revolt of Atahuallpa, even though it was precipitated by Huayna Ccapac's decision to divide the imperial power, was the breaking point and left Peru prostrate when the Pizarro expedition made an end to native independence.

Conclusion

The theme of this book has been The Golden Lands.
They coincide with the regions of high culture in ancient
America. Why they should also contain most of the sources of the
gold in the continent seems to have been an irrelevant question.
In Mexico and among the Maya gold was but little known before
the Toltec invasion in the late eighth century. Its presence added
beauty and glitter to many splendid objects, but it did nothing to
alter the nature of their civilizations. In Middle America and
northern South America there was plenty of gold before the
beginning of the Christian era. It formed part of the glory of
chieftainship and made many beautiful expressions of the arts
possible. Its highest social importance was in the land of the
Chibcha, around Bogotá in Colombia. Here the chief was truly the
Golden One, and gold was the symbol of human escape from the
deluge.

In Peru gold had been known from the second millennium BC,
and it was the ornament of gods and rulers, but the Incas made it
the symbol of the sun their ancestor, calling their great temple The
House of Gold. Here indeed was a land of gold.

To the Spaniards whose fortune it was to conquer all the lands
referred to in this book, the treasures which they took from the
Indies altered the face of Europe by financing the wars which the
Spanish Habsburgs used to dominate Europe and at the same time
to break the Turkish threat in central Europe.

But the gold accumulated for the glories of American chiefs was
sadly nearly all melted down for the conquerors. The beautiful
things we have today are buried treasures recovered from graves
and ruins, a faint echo of the treasure which once was beauty in
the eyes of men.

Appendix

IN THIS BOOK WE HAVE, TO AVOID CONFUSION, KEPT THE DATES
of pre-history in accordance with the generally accepted series of Carbon
14 determinations. But the recent discovery of the ancient bristle-cone
pine has enabled true dates based on tree-ring sequences to be taken
back to nearly 5000 BC. This has enabled us to escape the contradictions
in which Carbon 14 dates were increasingly more recent than historical
dates in the ancient Middle East. It appears that we must increase the
dates of objects from before the Christian era on a progressively
increasing scale. This scale differs a little for each year, so we cannot
count it as a smooth curve, but it is approximately so. The present state
of affairs is that dates of around 1000 BC should be increased by about
two hundred years. By 1500 BC the error has become a little in excess of
three hundred years; by 3000 BC it has become nearly eight hundred years,
and by 5000 BC it is a thousand years too late when counted on a Carbon
14 scale. Thus it means that all the earlier dates in this book have to be
extended by an appropriate amount, though the extension in the
Christian era is practically nil.

There is still much discussion in scientific circles about the reason for
this aberration in the Carbon 14 dating system; but the change derived
from the tree-ring dating has reconciled the differences found among the
historical dates of Egyptian and Babylonian material when compared to
the much more recent Carbon 14 dates obtained for the same material.
The change, of course, affects all materials from a context where there is
no definite historical date available. This includes all our ancient
American material.

A Short Bibliography

EARLY SOURCES

de Ayala, Felipe Huaman Poma: *Nueva Coronica y Buen Gobierno*, facsimile edition (Paris, Institut d'Ethnologie, 1936).

de Landa, Diego: *The Things of Yucatan* (English Translation).

Diaz del Castillo, Bernal: *True History of the Things of New Spain* (Harmondsworth. Pelican, 1963).

Sahagún, Fray Bernardino de: *General History of the Things of New Spain* (School of American Research & University of Utah, Salt Lake City, 1960–70).

Cieza de Leon, Pedro: *The Incas of Pedro Cieza de Leon* (Norman, 1959).

MORE RECENT WORKS

Basler, Adolphe, and Brummer, Ernest: *L'Art Precolombienne* (Paris, 1928).

Bennett, Wendell C: *Ancient Arts of the Andes* (New York, 1954).

Bergsøe, Paul: *The Metallurgy and Technology of Gold and Platinum among the Precolombian Indians* (Copenhagen, 1937).

Bogotá, Museo de Oro Nacional: *Masterpieces from the Gold Museum* (Bogotá, 1954 and later edition).

Burland, Cottie A: *Magic Books from Mexico* (London, 1953).
The Gods of Mexico (London, 1967).
The People of the Ancient Americas (Feltham, 1970).
Montezuma (London, 1973).

Bushnell, Geoffrey H. S: *Peru* (London, 1963).

Bushnell, G. H. S. and Digby, Adrian: *Ancient American Pottery* (London, 1955).

Caso, Alfonso: *The Aztecs, People of the Sun* (Oklahoma, 1958).

Collier, Donald: *Survey and Excavations in Southern Ecuador* (Chicago, 1943).

Covarrubias, Miguel: *Indian Art of Mexico and Central America* (New York, 1957).

Cruxent, Jose, and Rouse, Irving: *An Archaeological Chronology of Venezuela* (Washington, 1958–9).

d'Harcourt, Raoul: *Primitive Art of the Americas* (Paris, 1950).

Dockstader: *Indian Art of Central America* (London, 1954).
South American Indian Art (London, 1967).

Ford, James A: *Excavations in the Vicinity of Cali, Colombia* (New Haven, 1944).

Hagen, Victor von: *Highway of the Sun* (New York, 1957).

Hemming, J: *The Conquest of the Incas* (London, 1970).

Huxley, M. and Capa, C: *Farewell to Eden* (London, 1965).

Hyams, E. and Ordish, G: *The Last of the Incas* (London, 1963).

Joyce, Thomas Athol: *Mexican Archaeology* (London, 1914).
  South American Archaeology (London, 1912).

Kendall, Ann: *Everyday Life of the Incas* (London, 1973).

Kubler, George: *Art and Architecture of Ancient America* (Harmondsworth, 1962).

Lanning, E: *Peru Before the Incas* (Englewood Cliffs, 1967).

Lanning, E. and others: *Prehispanic America* (London, 1974).

Leon Portilla, Miguel: *The Broken Spears, Aztec Accounts of the Conquest* (London, 1962).

Longyear, John M. III: *Archaeological Excavations in El Salvador* (Cambridge, 1944).

Lothrop, Samuel Kirkland: *Archaeology of Southern Veraguas, Panama* (Cambridge, 1950).
  Coclé, an Archaeological Study of Central Panama (Cambridge, 1937 and 1942).
  Treasures of Ancient America (New York, 1964).

Mason, J. Alden: *The Ancient Civilizations of Peru* (Harmondsworth, 1957).
  Costa Rican Stonework (New York, 1945).

Moser, B. and Taylor, D: *The Cocaine Eaters* (London, 1965).

Nicholson, Irene: *Mexican and Central American Mythology* (Feltham, 1967).
  Firefly in the Night (London, 1959).

Osborne, Harold: *South American Indian Mythology* (Feltham, 1968).

Osgood, Cornelius and Howard, George D: *An Archaeological Survey of Venezuela* (New Haven, 1943).

Perez de Barradas, Jose: *El Arte Rupestre en Colombia* (Madrid, 1941).

Soustelle, Jacques: *Daily Life of the Aztecs* (Harmondsworth, 1961).

Stone, Doris Z: *Introduction to the Archaeology of Costa Rica* (San José, 1958).

Tax, Sol: *Civilizations of Ancient America* (Chicago, 1951).

Thompson, Sir J. Eric S: *The Rise and Fall of Maya Civilization* (London, 1956).

Vaillant, George C: *The Aztecs of Mexico* (Harmondsworth, 1952).

Acknowledgments

The author and publisher would like to thank the following museums, institutions and photographers for supplying the illustrations reproduced on the pages listed below:

Ferdinand Anton 2, 17, 23, 47, 48 (top and bottom), 48–9, 49 (bottom), 51, 56, 57, 58, 61, 63, 66–7, 69, 71, 73, 76–7, 85, 86, 89, 90, 92, 93, 94, 96, 97, 98, 99, 106, 108, 109, 112–13, 114, 116, 117, *119*, 123, 124, 126, 131, 145, 146, 148–9, 154, 155, 156, 158, 159, 163, 164, *169*, 172, 175, 176, 185, 186, 189, 195, 197, 199, 202, 206, 208, 213, 218, 219, 229, 231; Archaeological Museum, Cuzco, 227; Douglas Botting 224; British Museum 80–1, *102*, 142, 152, *179*, 217, 221; Brooklyn Museum, New York, 56, 57; Camera Press Ltd 35, 224; Collection Señor Mujica Gallo *191*; Werner Forman Archive, 33, *41*, *42–3*, *44*, *101*, *102*, *120*, 127, 144, *170*, *182*, 205, 210, 211; Giraudon 94, 104; Stephen Harrison 8, 25, 26, 31, 133; Michael Holford Library *179*, *180*, *181*, *191*, 209; Eugen Kusch 19, 38, 194, 214, 227; Linden Museum, Stuttgart 90; Museum of the American Indian, New York, 205, 211; Museo de la Universidad Veracruzana, 63, 71; Museum für Volkerkunde, Berlin 69; Museum für Volkerkunde, Munich 209; National Museum of Anthropology, Mexico, 51, 94, 98, 104, 127; Corporation of Nottingham Art Museum 177; Radio Times Hulton Picture Library 111; Museum voor Land en Volkenkunde en Maritiem Museum 'Prins Hendrik', Rotterdam 150, 161; Bernard C. Silberstein 35; Dr Kurt Stavenhagen Collection 33, *44*; Textile Museum, Washington D.C. 189; Robert Harding Associates, *192*.

Numbers in italics indicate colour illustrations.

Picture research by Pat Hodgson.
The maps on pages 6 and 7 designed by Tony Garrett.

Index